SAGE was founded in 1965 by Sara Miller McCune to support the dissemination of usable knowledge by publishing innovative and high-quality research and teaching content. Today, we publish over 900 journals, including those of more than 400 learned societies, more than 800 new books per year, and a growing range of library products including archives, data, case studies, reports, and video. SAGE remains majority-owned by our founder, and after Sara's lifetime will become owned by a charitable trust that secures our continued independence.

Los Angeles | London | New Delhi | Singapore | Washington DC | Melbourne

ADVANCE PRAISE

Strategic Brilliance admonishes the basic criteria which we associate with brilliance. This makes us realize that brilliance shines through all the coverings to make a profound impact and, in that, it solves the right problem. That is what brilliance is about. It is a fabulously crafted conclusion of what it really means to be brilliant. It is a must-read for business leaders.

Dilip Desai, *Chairman, Baker Tilly India*

Chetan Walia has brought out some of the key aspects for value creation using creativity, well-thought-out plans and execution. Some of the topics and discussion such as mediocrity to brilliance, everything is a decision and creativity is central to success really play a big role in building strong businesses. He has also brought out the importance of defining a culture, in addition to highlighting how obsession can create legacy disorder. He has also very aptly touched upon the momentum effect. I remember how motion plays a role in physics, which I am glad that Chetan has brought as a part of the book in driving brilliance rather than excellence for creating varying business models. It is a great read, great learning and wonderful recall to the core values that one should possess while building firms and leading them to success.

A. Balasubramanian, *MD and CEO,*
Aditya Birla Sun Life Mutual Fund

The world is witnessing contradictory trends. On the one side, big is becoming bigger and strong is becoming stronger. On the other side, an idea can disrupt structures and challenge leaders. Innovation and creativity are likely to be the differentiator and the biggest driver of value creation in the future. *Strategic Brilliance* brings out a great framework for value creation through creativity.

Nilesh Shah, *Managing Director, Kotak AMC*

Thought-provoking and insightful, *Strategic Brilliance* brings in a fresh perspective to a lot of management gospels. The book is so counter-intuitive that it makes you pause, think and reflect, and then leaves you contemplating that brilliance, eventually, is so simple. It is a must-read for any new-age thinker!

Nikhil Kamath, *Co-founder, Zerodha and True Beacon*

It is truly a riveting discourse on strategies for success in the world of business. It gives a unique take and raises some poignant questions through the use of everyday conversations, newspaper headlines and childhood tales. It is an impeccable piece of work for future business leaders, managers, bureaucrats, academicians and students. It definitely struck a chord with me, a must-read!

Pawan K. Kumar (IRS), *Deputy Managing Director,*
India Infrastructure Finance Company Limited

STRATEGIC BRILLIANCE

SAGE Response, our business books imprint, celebrates its silver jubilee this year. As we reflect on this transformational journey that began with a single title, we thank everyone who has helped us to produce content that is topical and relevant across a varied audience of aspiring managers, working professionals, practitioners and students. We feel privileged that eminent management and leadership experts, professionals and stalwarts from academia supported and trusted us with their work. Over the years, SAGE Response has built an enviable list of practice-based, reader-friendly books that provide creative strategies to keep pace with the rapidly changing global scenario. As we grow and evolve with the times, it is our endeavour to continue to publish books that offer innovative solutions, approaches and perspectives to the disciplines that we serve.

STRATEGIC
BRILLIANCE

FROM CONCEPT
TO REALITY

CHETAN WALIA

Los Angeles | London | New Delhi
Singapore | Washington DC | Melbourne

First published in 2022 by

SAGE Publications India Pvt Ltd
B1/I-1 Mohan Cooperative Industrial Area
Mathura Road, New Delhi 110 044, India
www.sagepub.in

SAGE Publications Inc
2455 Teller Road
Thousand Oaks, California 91320, USA

SAGE Publications Ltd
1 Oliver's Yard, 55 City Road
London EC1Y 1SP, United Kingdom

SAGE Publications Asia-Pacific Pte Ltd
18 Cross Street #10-10/11/12
China Square Central
Singapore 048423

Published by Vivek Mehra for SAGE Publications India Pvt Ltd. Typeset in 11.5/14.5pt Bembo by Fidus Design Pvt Ltd, Chandigarh.

Library of Congress Control Number: 2021944071

ISBN: 978-93-5479-135-2 (PB)

SAGE Team: Namarita Kathait, Shipra Pant, Anoushka Gupta and Anupama Krishnan

*To everyone who wonders
if I am writing about my experiences with them.*
I am.

CONTENTS

ACKNOWLEDGEMENTS

Thanks to Ma for being patient with my prolonged bouts of silence. Thanks to Gunu for always being present and sensitive. Thanks to Heena for being there and aware while I remained oblivious to everything around. Thanks to Aayra for being so brave. I am so proud of you. Thanks to Lonna for letting me write this book before I write hers. Thanks to Rolly for being my thinking partner and being always available to listen to all the crazy ideas.

I also want to thank every organization that I have worked or consulted with. That experience of associating with them has gone into almost every chapter in this book. Then there is a list of people, some I know and some I have never known, but I have drawn inspiration from them in some very meaningful ways. They are as follows:

Ashok Ranchchod	Mihaly Csikszentmihalyi
Bharat Goenka	O. P. Sharma
Clayton Christensen	Rajiv Prasad
David McClelland	Steve Jobs
D. H. Groberg	Thomas and Kilman
Eliyahu M. Goldratt	Viju Parameshwar
Hellen Keller	Walt Disney
John Nash	Zig Ziglar
Lev Vygotsky	

INTRODUCTION

Every single discovery and creation begins at first with an observation. In the academic world, the observation takes the form of an empirical research. In business, it takes the form of entrepreneurship. Eventually, everything becomes obvious and just hindsight.

I have been working with and closely observing some of the largest companies in the world. I have also been closely working with and observing the academic world. It has been intriguing to me how theory and practice develop almost in isolation and yet feed off each other.

This book is an integration of perspectives that I gathered in my work as an academic theorist and with the experience I gained as a business consultant over the last two decades. Along this journey of working in and with business leaders, I have seen two recessions, two extreme bubble bursts, multiple breakthroughs, disruptions, strategic makeovers—yet, the discoveries I made alongside my team remained extraordinarily successful and profitable for the organizations I partnered with.

This book has something very new and staggeringly different to say about building, running and growing businesses. A lot of clients or leaders we meet are sometimes sceptical about the way we perceive organizations, and sometimes they are overtly intimidated about the depth we bring to the table. Oftentimes, business leaders feel overwhelmed in working with us. Yet every single company and leader who has worked with us has experienced a breakthrough. The method has never failed, be it in a recession or in a boom.

Some businesses we approach, of course, choose not to work with us and choose bigger consulting brands instead. Some have even called us too creative and too far ahead of reality.

Our take is that critics do not really understand how companies can reject popular knowledge, best practices, tried and tested formulas, leadership theories and experiences, and actually, in doing so, achieve breakthroughs. They don't understand any of it. It's their problem, really, not mine. Sometimes businesses have a false sense of security because they feel that they have the best of the minds from the Big Four working for them. Screw that. Because so did every Fortune 500 company that no longer exists.

They seem to think that strategic success lies in execution. They're wrong. In our experience, execution is a default outcome of clarity.

They say that values-based management is the key to longevity and sustained success. They're wrong. We have proven, and as you'll read ahead, authenticity is the key and not inauthentic posters. They believe that accuracy of decision-making depends upon the intelligence of interpreting data. Wrong again. Decisions and data have often nothing to do with each other.

Innovation has often been assumed to be the exceptional ability or a complicated structural change to achieve. They say that cultural limitations limit innovative capabilities. But we have always achieved the opposite.

They seem to think that excellence is what everything must strive for and build. We believe and as you'll see shortly, excellence is the enemy of brilliance.

Popular methods, theories and beliefs say a whole lot. They are mostly wrong and, when right, they are at best mediocre. I have experienced it over and over again. And therefore, I wrote this book to show you how you can experience it too.

The book will not criticize or put anyone down. I will first take you to the very fundamentals of how and what we think, value and perceive. You will identify with the baggage and burden of these false narratives. From there on, we will together build a common sense understanding of creative and strategic thinking. We will put, in context, the real virtues of culture, execution and potential. Finally, I hope to arrive with you at your strategic brilliance.

Now, let's get to it.

STAGE ONE

THINKING
BRILLIANCE

FALSE NARRATIVE

THINK
BIG!

THE FALSE NARRATIVE OF SUCCESS

Success isn't all about thinking big!

From Walt Disney to Richard Branson, from Henry Ford to Bill Gates and from Edison to Buffet, we think that their success stories were linear. All it took was a big idea and their capacity to think big!

Thinking big has been drilled down deep into our minds.

The biographical accounts of the remarkable leaders of the past and the present lead us to an assumption that it all begins with thinking big. After all, almost every high achiever says so, at least in hindsight. Did thinking big take them there? Sure enough one must think big, but does that do anything by itself?

Thinking big is usually understood as being wildly ambitious. It is equated to imagining a great future and then taking steps towards that. As a child, everyone has built castles in the air. That doesn't mean that every child became Superman, flying around as the saviour of the world.

Anyone can think big. And everyone, at some point in their lives, has thought big. It has led to more heartbreaks than breakthroughs. The castles people build for themselves don't translate into a reality for over 99 per cent of the world's population.

A few years ago, I was sitting across the chairman of one of the most well-known retail groups. An hour into the conversation, this man told me that he'd checked into a hotel thrice in the last 10 years with the intent of killing himself. This is one of the most well-respected, visionary, self-made leaders. Thinking big drove him to doing big things. The thinking, though, doesn't have a full stop. For some reason, imagination seems to run out. Thereafter, doing big becomes about deviant strategies, trickery and money play, over and above creating value. In the end, no one seems to thrive or survive in the Red Queen's race.

Einstein once wrote a preface for a book where he noted that imagination is more important than knowledge. In research for this book, people who were generally regarded as geniuses were studied. There is a very intriguing discovery that must be shared with you. Henri Poincaré, the eminent French mathematician, wrote, 'Logic has very little to do with discovery.' Karl Popper, the renowned Austrian scientific philosopher, wrote, 'Every discovery contains a creative intuition.' Einstein wrote about the aspects of science, 'There is no logical way to discovery of these elemental laws. There is only the way of intuition.' Finally, Nobel Prize-winning mathematician John Nash said, 'Rational thought imposes limitations.' He believed that the periods of 'enforced rationality', imposed by the medical treatments he received for treating schizophrenia, were detrimental to his imagination.

Logic, rationality and thought, of course, have their place. However, the words from eminent achievers, the ones who have changed the world in many ways, suggest that their perceptions and achievements have little to do with their thoughts. Thinking, big or small, is a result of our past knowledge and experiences. Thus, most of the times, we act as we think. But the actions don't always translate into sustained or expected results. Was it the thinking that was wrong? Or is the knowledge it is based upon incorrect?

Or could it be that thinking in itself is just a low-level inaccurate activity?

RED QUEEN RACE

THE STRUGGLE TO FIND STRATEGIC RELEVANCE

Less than 5 per cent of corporations in America's S&P 500 or Britain's FT 100 are able to maintain shareholder returns in the top quartile of their peers (Williamson, 2006).

Out of 18 companies that were singled out as visionary in the bestseller *Built to Last*, only 6 managed to outperform the Dow Jones Industrial Average (Hamel & Välikangas, 2003). This basically implies that the A-List companies of yesterday are merely a part of the crowd today. In a survey of over 500 CEOs, the majority expressed a concern that strategies of competing firms have become more alike, rather than different from one another (Williamson, 2006). This explains why the other 12 companies such as Disney, Motorola, Ford and Sony are no longer considered as great but just okay.

Lifespan of companies in S&P 500 has shrunk from around 60 years in 1960 to 16 years in 2010 (McGrath & Kim, 2015). This means that when a new firm is added, one is removed in every two weeks. Similarly, FTSE 100 in London churns out 15 per cent of its index each year.

The reality is no different for family-held businesses. Only 14 per cent of these businesses survive past the second generation and only 3 per cent beyond the third.

A recent study showed that over 90 per cent of start-ups simply never take off or make any money.

These realities force companies to enter a Red Queen's race. Lewis Carroll in her classic narrative, *Alice's Adventures in Wonderland*, narrated a little interaction between the queen and Alice. It's called the Red Queen effect (Carroll, 1946).

From the Red Queen effect, we learn how all strategic advantages are cancelled out by increasing competition. In other words, strategies that generated revenue for a firm cease to be unique. It takes all the running one can possibly do and yet remain at the same place where one began. Almost no one sustains strategic relevance in the Red Queen's race. In the end, only losers remain.

The Red Queen Effect

'Now! Now!' cried the queen. 'Faster! Faster!' And they went so fast at last that they seemed to skim through the air, hardly touching the ground with their feet tall; suddenly, just as Alice was getting quite exhausted, they stopped and she found herself sitting on the ground, breathless and giddy.

The queen popped her up against a tree and said kindly, 'You may rest a little now.'

Alice looked round at her in great surprise. 'Why, I do believe we've been under this tree the whole time! Everything's just as it was!'

'Of course, it is,' said the queen. 'What would you have it?'

'Well, in our country,' said Alice, still panting a little, 'you'd generally get to somewhere else, if you ran fast for a long time, as we've been doing.'

'A slow sort of country!' said the queen. 'Now, here, you see, it takes all the running you can do to keep in the same place. If you want to get somewhere else, you must run at least twice as fast as that!'

TRAINED
TO BE EXCELLENT
BUT NOT
BRILLIANT

TRAINED NOT TO BE BRILLIANT

Our education, expertise, skills and training educate us, at best, to be excellent in our chosen fields. They don't educate us to be brilliant. While excellence is the quality of being extremely good at something, brilliance is an exceptional ability. What makes brilliance even more difficult to decipher is that the brilliant minds of our generation have also not been able to articulate their own brilliance. You see, they aren't excellent narrators. Take, for instance, the brilliant minds such as Walt Disney, Steve Jobs and Warren Buffet or even Mahatma Gandhi, Nelson Mandela and Mother Teresa—we know that they were brilliant and produced remarkable breakthroughs which has changed the world in many ways. What we don't know is how to produce that brilliance and, so perhaps, we assume that we must begin by thinking big.

Imagine for a moment that a teacher in a school came across a student in her early years with an exceptional oratory ability—witty, talkative, has a reply to almost anything, has a natural talent to hold bold conversations, though has very little perfection in her academic work. What will happen? It is evident, isn't it? There will be pressure on the child to be excellent, and she will be encouraged or even punished when she's trying to be brilliant. This happens all the time. I have seen this very closely with my daughter when she was four. She was the wittiest kid I had ever known, and just two months into a fun playschool, I saw a kid who was more terrified of teachers than I had ever seen anyone be. That usually tends to be the beginning for conformity training. In a corporate setting, from there on, our companies design wonderful systems to reward such excellence.

Imagine for a moment what the world would look like if Einstein had embraced excellence in school when he was being pushed to, if Edison, who had never attended school and was encouraged to be a free spirit by his mother, was taken over and put into a disciplined schooling regime, if Ford was discouraged from making an imperfect automobile and if the Wright brothers had only focused on making their cycle business excellent.

Expertise or excellence is needed to execute, yes. But will expertise acknowledge the exception or disregard it? Sadly and mostly in our companies, the experts view it as a treasured managerial skill to convert the artist into an artisan. Think about it; if you visited Earth as an alien, you might have to conclude that the whole purpose of our corporate hierarchies and leadership structures must be to produce conformists who compete with each other to excel—to become excellent workers and not brilliant thinkers.

Take the example of Gillian Lynne (success of *Cats* and *The Phantom of the Opera*) whose mother became increasingly worried because the child found it impossible to sit and concentrate in class. The modern-day diagnosis for such a child would be hyperactive ADHD. However, in 1970, a specialist told the mother, 'Gillian isn't sick. She's a dancer. Let her just dance.' The rest is history. Isn't it worrying that a majority of specialists today would put this child on medication for calming down? And why? Because they are experts and they know better. Don't they?

BUMBLEBEE

IT FLIES!

INTELLIGENT IGNORANCE

There is a very popular Harvard experiment started in the 1950s spanning about 10 years from then on. It has been very decisive in its conclusions and very much relevant to us today.

For the experiment, researchers at Harvard chose people with very high IQ levels and possibly very high egos—the best of the best with PhDs. It was carried out with multiple groups of people with 10–15 people in each group. In it, Harvard's own collaborators were also included in each group to help the experiment.

Two sheets of paper were shown to the group. The first sheet had three bars—each very different in height. The other sheet had one bar, matching one of the bars in the other sheet. It was very evident as to which one it matched. Unless one was blind, it should take a millisecond to answer. The sheets were shown to the crowd and the question was then asked—which bar does it match: left, middle or right?

The collaborators of the experiment were asked first and were already briefed to answer incorrectly. The three collaborators gave the same incorrect answer, first up. Then the rest of the group was asked.

In 90 per cent of the cases, the person was saying the wrong answer to follow the herd and be part of the majority. Ninety per cent! These are big IQ people. The Red Queen effect traps them too.

Brilliance is an exception, not the norm. You can't follow your way to brilliance.

Take the life of Hellen Keller, for example. She couldn't see, couldn't hear and was mute. One must believe in such a situation that life is over. Yet she was an incredible author. She was an active voice in political opinions. She lived a long life. She is as admired as any philosopher has been. How?

Desire must be combined with intelligent ignorance. Ignore what you don't have, rather than setting it as a benchmark for achievement.

A great example of intelligent ignorance is of bumblebee. It's impossible for a bumblebee to fly. The body is too heavy and the wings are too light. Any study you read on the bumblebee will prove this in any way you want. But you see, bumblebee doesn't read, it flies.

Henry Ford didn't go to school nor to college. He wasn't an engineer. He built the V8 engine. Edison had only three months of schooling in his entire life. He is the greatest inventor the world has seen. Google, Apple, Netflix, Amazon and Microsoft—the darling companies of the modern day—all have something in common with Ford, Edison, Einstein, Gandhi, Teresa and alike. They didn't start their businesses trying to beat someone out or in an attempt to satiate a moneymaking desire. They ignored all of that and focused on solving a problem. The rest were mere effects.

WHAT WOULD YOU DO?

THE ORANGE PROBLEM

NO BIG PICTURE AND NO BRILLIANCE IN OUTTHINKING

A classic negotiation problem was conceived by Follett (1940). It is known as the orange problem. Mr O was running a business empire, The Orange Company Inc. The Orange Company was the largest producer of oranges in the world. The business produced and sold various kinds of orange juices, fresh and packaged. Mr O was on the verge of retirement and was looking to pass on the baton to one of his two daughters. Both daughters were asked to present their vision of the future to the board chaired by Mr O.

The elder daughter, considered to be the frontrunner, was a board loyalist. She made her presentation on how the juice business will evolve and spread to other countries, how they will globalize the company and its mission, and how she, who understands the company's values, culture and ethos, is the right person to guide the team into the future.

The younger daughter was a challenger. She questioned the sustainability of the juice business amid growing competition. She questioned the resistance of the company's culture to innovation. She proposed that the company reduces its exposure to juice and uses its oranges to begin manufacturing the more profitable marmalades. She reasoned that it has a longer shelf life and will reduce the prevalent wastage of oranges in the company. Being a visionary, she stated that she would be the one to guide The Orange Company into the future.

Should Mr O go with the elder's view as it is safe and predictable? Should Mr O go with the challenger's big thinking view? Should he find a middle ground? How would you settle the conflict?

No big picture emerges from either one's big thinking. Thinking big is not the big picture. If the traditionalist view dominates, it will lead to an evolutionary strategy. The system will evolve, become a better version of itself and probably grow. Conversely, the challengers will, at best, revolutionize the system into an opposite of sorts. There will be lots of ideas, activities and an emergence of a new order. Effectively, the game will shift from the one over to the other. For example, if Mr O were to decide in favour of the younger daughter, the power will shift to the challenger.

The challengers in this manner will become the new traditionalists, guarding their own turf. All that happens here is a distributive effect. The game shifts from one to the other. This is the distributive dimension. As systems evolve, power shifts from one to the other or market shares may shift from one to the other. The distributive dimension is a natural occurrence between the traditionalists and challengers. It adds nothing to value creation. It's merely a shift. It will shift again, just like the exchange of power in democratically elected governments.

The other dimension is the protective dimension. For example, Mr O could feel the pressure from both the daughters and do nothing. He could sit back and wait for the conflict to resolve by itself or wait for the daughters to come to a consensus. Unfortunately, many people believe in this way of doing business. They feel that it will just go away. The protective dimension which tries to protect itself from both the traditionalists and the challengers leads to stagnation. Neither side is able to effectively carry out a vision, causing the system to collapse. The industry-level pulls and pushes between the gatekeepers and challengers ensure that most companies eventually collapse or stagnate. The giants like Kodak make way for the modern-day superstar. The superstar becomes today's gatekeeper. Somewhere in a garage, a young challenging mind may already be planning the next disruption.

There is no brilliance in outthinking the other. It is just a transient shift from a gatekeeper to the challenger.

Fatal Error

 YOU PRECISELY SOLVED THE WRONG PROBLEM

[OK]   [Cancel]

ERROR OF THE THIRD KIND

Error of the third kind is usually understood as the error by providing the right answer to the wrong problem (Barbara & Mitroff, 2014). Mathematician Richard Hamming expressed his view that 'It is better to solve the right problem the wrong way than to solve the wrong problem the right way.'

It is this problem perception that plagues brilliance. Thinking big usually leads to a problem of comparisons: the gap between aspirations and reality. Is that even a problem or is that a reality in itself? We spend our careers, create businesses, hire the best talent and use precious resources to precisely solve the wrong problem. Businesses succeed as well. They generate wealth. But then it disappears into the distributive dimension because someone else outwitted you at being even more precise in solving the wrong problem.

Businesses, even the most established ones, fall into the trap of the third kind error all the time. The managing director of a $2 billion company that I coach was narrating his most pressing problem to me. He said that his problems would be solved if everyone in his company were to just align and collaborate. On probing further, my team discovered that alignment meant aligning to the dominant views and collaboration meant to stop criticizing or challenging these views and work in that manner. Most people have jobs to save and would probably end up aligning. This is the decision-making syndrome we'll specifically explore in Stage 6. However, this is an example of solving the wrong or an assumed problem.

It is astounding the number of times I have heard the words 'alignment' from the top decision-makers. Although they use the word 'alignment' to solve most of their problems, what they actually mean is to 'follow the herd'.

Business leaders often fall into the trap of knowledge and experience. They tend to believe that they are best poised to read situations. At times they might as well be, however, all experience and knowledge can, at best, be a path to excellence, right? The reluctance to open out to opposing views often causes leaders to inadvertently make errors of the third kind. Leaders tend to assume that opposing views will create a revolution that they will not be able to manage. The opposing view, of course, represents a revolution, and no business wants to deal with a fight. So we continue to persist with the error of the third kind because we don't have the brilliance to craft the whole picture. We get stuck with our assumptions that stop us from looking at the bigger picture.

THE WHOLE

PICTURE

BRILLIANCE LIES IN THE WHOLE PICTURE

There is another dimension in the conflict between the traditionalists and the challengers. It is the wholistic dimension. This is not one versus the other. This is one and the other. Take a look at Figure 1.1.

Figure 1.1 presents five infliction points. Point A is the point of stagnation. Point B is the evolution or the victory of gatekeepers. Point C is the revolution or the victory of challengers. The distance between points B and C is the distributive dimension. Point D is the compromise between points B and C. The distance between points D and A represents the protective

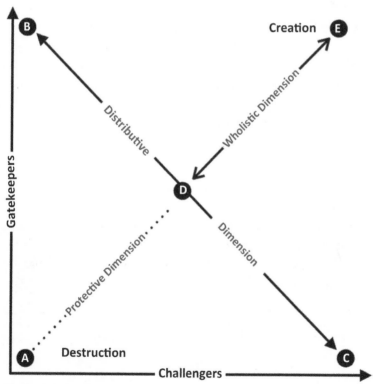

Figure 1.1 Dimensions of Different Perspectives

dimension. There is a point E that integrates the traditionalists and the challengers. This is the wholistic dimension, which is the creative dimension. This is the only dimension where total value creation takes place and brilliance operates.

Traditionalists are excellent at their jobs like Mr O's elder daughter. The challengers are also excellent at their jobs like Mr O's younger daughter. Brilliance is the exceptional ability to perceive this reality that both are excellent. Brilliance is the ability to combine and integrate the traditionalists and the challengers, so that there is creation and not mere distribution.

Not so long ago in India, one of the largest business houses, Reliance Group, was in the same precarious position as Mr O. The difference was that Mr O was no longer there, and the two potential successors wanted control of the business. The mediators found a middle ground across the distributive dimension and divided the business into two. The challenger virtually stands collapsed. That's destruction. The gatekeeper thrived and is one of the largest companies in India. That's evolution. Creation is what Mr O did in our story.

The gatekeeper or the elder daughter wanted to take the legacy of the juice business forward. The challenger or younger one wanted to invent the new marmalade business. Mr O didn't divide. He integrated. The pulps of the oranges were taken over by the elder daughter to produce juice. The wasted juice and the peel of the oranges, which were of no use to the existing business model, were taken over by the younger daughter to manufacture marmalade.

Brilliance solves the right problem.

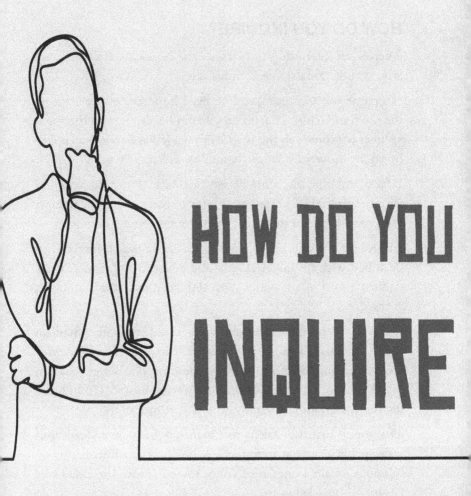

HOW DO YOU INQUIRE

HOW DO YOU INQUIRE?

There is an interesting story about the legendary Italian Count who was the greatest lover of his age.

His name was Casanova, and he lived hundreds of years ago in the town of Genoa. Legend says that in his day, he was the finest seducer of women in the world. His name has become a euphemism for those who fancy themselves as lady's men.

I have not known a lot about this man. I've told you just about everything I know about him in the previous paragraph. However, there is a story that goes around about Casanova.

At around the age of 80, Count Casanova was laying on his deathbed with his butler, doctor and priest in attendance. Weak and close to death, Casanova was disturbed by a loud knocking at the door.

His butler went to the door and was greeted by a young Scottish youth who said, 'I must see Casanova. I have travelled for three weeks, and only he can answer my question.' The butler told him that it was not possible, but the young man insisted. Upon hearing the commotion, Casanova yelled, 'Let him in.'

The young man was taken to Casanova's bedside, and without waiting for a formal introduction, he launched into his pitch. 'Casanova, I am a big fan of yours. You see, I love the ladies too. I want to be a lady's man but don't know the best way to go about it. I hear you've been with over 1000 women and I hope to do the same. What's your secret? I know you have one and I would love to have it too.'

Casanova, gravely ill and near the end of his life, beckoned him to come over, then grabbed the boy's collar and pulled the young man's ear close to his mouth and said, 'It's easy. I asked them.'

The Casanova story challenges the young man's assumption that there must be a secret. In strategic terms, this is called the defining error. Defining error is working on the wrong problem. This will nullify all the actions we take to solve the problem. The defining error leads to an implementing error; that is, the solutions that emerge will not be put to effective use. This will nullify all the previous steps. Just like the Red Queen's race, after all this activity, one remains at the same starting position. These two errors represent the most complex aspects of strategic problem management: the nature of cause and effect (defining problems) and the dynamic nature of human beings (implementing solutions).

Normally, companies engage in one of the two systems of inquiry to arrive at their construct of strategic challenges that they must solve. Technically or academically, these are called the Lockean and Hegelian inquiring systems. For ease of understanding, we'll call these the inliers and outliers. Both these systems simply represent different ways of arriving at the 'truth' about anything. They don't necessarily represent the correct or right way to define or solve a problem.

In the inlier approach, the truth is based on agreement. A clear majority in the group signals an agreement or a decision. The majority is correct, and the deviant members are wrong. The extremes are viewed as distractions. Inliers ignore the extreme views. All they need is to arrive at an agreement, and the system runs through all groups in the organization. People arrive at an agreement and tend to believe that they are right. The minority group is usually convinced, or at least silenced, by the fact that the majority has found the truth.

The second approach is the outlier approach. Truth is determined by disagreement. The same situation is viewed differently by different people. The focus is on the extreme positions to understand why people see that situation differently. All aspects of the problems may come to the fore and become accessible. The outlier system takes the time to listen to the extreme views. By taking time to learn, a complex problem can be understood. There tends to be a greater understanding and confidence after the members have considered all perspectives. The members tend to get used to or be at ease with complexity.

EXCELLENCE

KILLS

BRILLIANCE

EXCELLENCE KILLS BRILLIANCE

It is now possible to see how the traditionalists and challengers can get locked into their extreme positions. Both the positions are honed over years of gathering knowledge, experience and information. Each position represents excellence in its own way. For example, in Mr O's story, both the ideas had excellent merit. However, in the distributive dimension between the gatekeepers and challengers, each gets focused on 'my point' versus 'your point'. Each is a position of thinking big. Each is a position of respective truths. Even then, no matter where you agree on the distribution dimension, the effect on total value creation will be minimal. It will remain distributed.

Traditionalists represent the inlier's views and challengers represent the outlier's views. In most systems or companies, either end of this may have the final say. Companies usually adopt both the outlier and inlier methods. Having listened to the extreme views, the decision-makers will usually apply the inlier system and drive a majority opinion that suits them. In certain cases, where the challengers are equally powerful, the agreement may occur along the outlier dimension.

No matter who wins, the brilliance is lost. Excellence is the norm. If one is diligent and sincere enough in following the rules laid down by the education system, one will most certainly acquire excellence. Brilliance is the exception. In the battle of traditionalists and challengers, essentially two differing positions of excellence, combined with our comparative desires to do better than the other—the integrative possibilities of brilliance—are usually killed.

It is the nature of the world. We fight wars for dividing nations, territories, communities, local districts, companies, wealth and properties. None of this creates anything more than what was already there.

I was recently approached by a start-up who had spent over $10 million in getting market-ready. Their products are a line of luxury lifestyle products (furniture, light fixtures and artefacts). They created a physical platform for designers from all over the world to meet, collaborate and come up with some path-breaking work. Having created the design, the company went to handcraft each and every piece. The assumption the company made very early on is that they are in the luxury end of the market. This assumption drove everything from the choice of designers, raw materials, processes and retail outlets. Having spent $10 million, their operational expense requirement is $2 million annually. Their sales for the last two years combined were a mere $15,000. The products are great and instantly reso-nate with the viewer, but the viewer cannot become a customer because the products are unaffordable.

The challenging view of the company is to not be in a luxury segment but to mass produce so as to make the products have a wider reach. The decision-makers are so wedded to the luxury mindset that they would rather threaten the existence of the venture than integrate the opposite view.

The assumptions dictate the markets the business serves. The dictate the customers. The identify the competitors. They also determine the values and behaviours, not only of the company and its employees but also of its customers and ecosystem.

Assumptions are needed in any activity related to the future because we don't have perfect information about what the future may hold. Assumptions about the key stakeholders (internal and external) form a strategic reality for a business. Businesses get paid for servicing these assumptions. The strategic business drivers and custodians of these assumptions often fall into the trap of not thinking critically. The realities evolve and change, but assumptions do not.

Assumptions usually require to be challenged through the outlier inquiry system. Within companies, however, these assumptions are protected by the top teams through the inlier inquiry system. They all agree on the truth of the assumptions, so it must be true.

Kodak, Nokia, Blackberry, Woolworth and alike are prominent and much-quoted examples of how outdated assumptions led to the downfall of giants.

THE CHOICE IS NOT
THIS OR THAT

↓

AND

MR O'S BRILLIANCE

Extreme positions were stated by both the daughters. The most common approach is to divide the pie by two. That requires neither excellence nor brilliance.

The mind will take the course depending upon the intent perceived. Let us say that the intent is to become number one in the industry. Let us examine a real case that played out in the Indian aviation industry. The two market leaders, at one point in time, were Jet Airways and Kingfisher Airlines—both non-existent as you read this. Both, driven by the desire to be number one, made the exact same mistake. Kingfisher Airlines acquired Air Deccan which was running the opposite business model of low cost as compared to Kingfisher's full service model. Jet Airways acquired Sahara which in its final years was a run-down badly managed operation. Using the Sahara infrastructure, Jet Airways launched its low-cost version, Jet Konnect. Neither airline could recover from the conflicting demands of being seen as full service airline versus aspiring for the market shares of low-cost airlines. In compromising between the gatekeepers (existing model) and challengers (low-cost model), both airlines entered the protective dimension and destroyed themselves.

Mr O was faced with a similar problem but was guided by the intent of resolving the problem and not compromising on it. Mr O also bifurcated the business into juice and marmalade to create a win-win solution. Unlike Jet and Kingfisher, in this hypothetical story though, the same resources created additional value that didn't exist before. In the case of the airlines, the combined resources of four airlines and all the brains therein couldn't figure out what determines a strategic value. In the end, none of them exist anymore.

Brilliance requires an integrative solution which consists of an integrative inquiry approach and a combination of both inlier and outlier, but in the opposite direction of the norm. Take a look at Figure 5.2. Normally, once the extreme positions have been presented, we tend to apply the inlier approach to evolve an understanding across the distributive dimension. For example, in Mr O's case, the normal way may be to compromise or settle one versus the other.

This requires an integrative inquiry approach, a combination of both inlier and outlier, but in the opposite direction of the norm. Being brilliant is in asking and finding the answers to the question: How can we integrate the two extremes into creating value that is currently non-existent?

There were established companies in the recent coronavirus pandemic which were firing employees, cutting costs and reducing operational footprint to survive. These companies didn't have faith in their employees, systems and ways of working, that they will be able to manoeuvre their way out of the problem. They have never allowed problems to create value. Either you defeat the problem or the problem defeats you has been their mindset. And hence, such companies will always be the biggest losers in a moment of crisis.

Then there were companies who saw the problem and adjusted to it almost immediately. Apple was investing in opening stores in the emerging markets of India which were perceived to be somewhat immune to a global recession. Tesla was making ventilators. Alibaba was shipping medical supplies to every country. Amazon was negotiating with governments to schedule deliveries in lockdown. Netflix and YouTube were adjusting the streaming speeds to retain their user base. While airlines world over were cutting salaries, Boeing was utilizing its biggest aircrafts to rush medical supplies. While there were hotel chains that had virtually suspended operations and announced salary cuts, there were those that converted hotels into quarantine facilities.

Advertising business came to a standstill during lockdown and so did their creativity. People were consuming content on TV and social media more than ever, and no agency could figure out a way to work with clients to do something productive.

There were companies who lost brand equity, and there were companies who gained it. Every crisis leads to emergence of brilliance. Google and Apple survived the dot-com bubble to emerge as technology giants of the future. Alibaba survived the SARS scare to emerge as a global powerhouse.

Being brilliant is not about being a winner or a loser. It is not about defeating a problem. This is how comparative thinking mindsets work. Being brilliant is about understanding the problem. It is about acknowledging the conflict. It is about seeing the excellence in opposing views. Then brilliance emerges from the intent to create value by integrating factions into creations. Big thinking looks at the 'I' in comparison to the other and solves one's own problems of desire, but brilliance looks at the excellence of two or more 'Is' and integrates their big thinking into solving a real problem and creating value as a result of it. This requires a holistic understanding of the creative process.

BRILLIANCE CREDO: BEING BRILLIANT

At the end of each stage, this book presents you with reflective questions. These aren't merely for reflection. They serve a larger purpose. I urge you to answer these questions right after reaching the end of each stage. Your every answer will provide clarity to a point, where by the end of Stage 4 you will be clear about your strategically brilliant intent. By the end of this book, after the final stage, all your answers will come together to capture and create your own strategic brilliance blueprint.

1. What are the assumptions you have held about succeeding that seem to be self-defeating or non-value creating?

2. What do these assumptions need to be replaced with?

3. What method of inquiry have you predominantly used, inlier or outlier, and how has it restricted you from exploring brilliance?

4. Who are your main stakeholders, internal or external (e.g., competitors, governments, employees, vendors, society or family)?

5. What are your key assumptions (2–3) for each of these stakeholders? (The assumptions may be true or false. We are just examining assumptions).

6. Next to each assumption, please write the letter 'M' or 'L'. 'M' signifies most important and 'L' signifies least important. Least important means that if you are wrong about that particular assumption, it may not matter much to the overall goal. Most important means that if you are wrong about that particular assumption, you can no longer reach your goal.

7. Next to each assumption, write the letters 'C' or 'U'. 'C' signifies certainty and 'U' signifies uncertainty. Certainty is assumptions that you are sure are true. Uncertainty is assumptions that you aren't sure are true.

8. The assumptions that are marked by 'M' and 'U' represent the critical region. These are the most important assumptions and you are not sure if they are true. What does the critical region tell you about the conclusions you were drawing from these assumptions?

9. What new conclusions (about your goals, intent and direction) can you draw?

10. What are the thinking big goals that you may have had in life that stand challenged by the above? What are some of the brilliance goals that may be occurring in your mind?

REFERENCES

Barbara, V., & Mitroff, I. (2014). *Business strategies for a messy world: Tools for systemic problem-solving.* Palgrave Pivot.

Carroll, L. (1946). *Through the looking glass and what Alice found there.* Grosset & Dunlap.

Follett, M. P. (1940). Constructive conflict. In H. Metcalf & L. Urwick (Eds.), *Dynamic administration: The collected papers of Mary Parker Follett* (pp. 30–49). Routledge.

Hamel, G., & Välikangas, L. (2003). The quest for resilience. *Harvard Business Review, 81*(9), 52–63.

McGrath, R. G., & Kim, J. (2015). Innovation, strategy & hyper-competition. In M. Dodgson, D. M. Gann, & N. Phillips (Eds.), *The Oxford handbook of innovation management* (pp. 397–419). Oxford University Press.

Williamson, P. J. (2006). Strategy innovation. In D. O. Faulkner & A. Campbell (Eds.), *The Oxford handbook of strategy* (pp. 841–874). Oxford University Press.

STAGE TWO

CREATIVITY MEETS STRATEGY

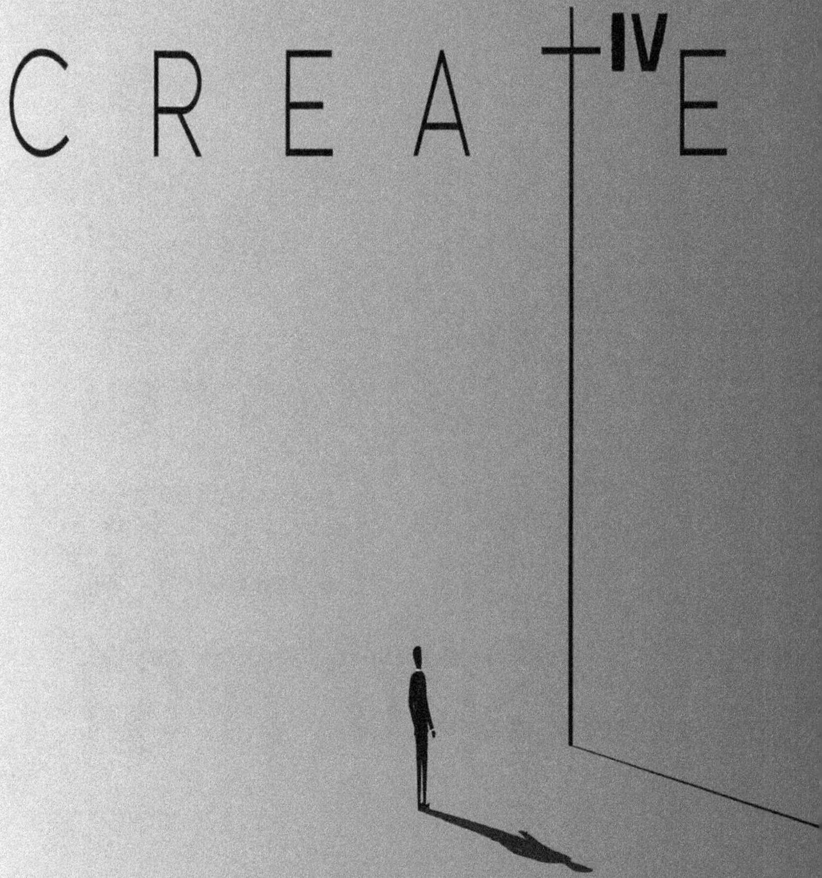
CREATIVE

CREATIVITY IS CENTRAL TO ECONOMIC SUCCESS

More than 50 per cent of economic growth in the 21st century came from products and services that were either in their infancy or did not exist at all in the 20th century (Dawson & Andriopoulos, 2017, 378). In a UNESCO (2015) report published in December 2015, the creative sector is estimated to generate US$2250 billion of revenue and 29.5 million jobs worldwide. Seventy per cent of leaders surveyed across a range of industries cite innovation as among their top three priorities of driving growth (Barsh et al., 2007).

What you think can be and cannot be and what you know is or would be seem to be more relevant in driving economic success. In other words, as Einstein said, 'Knowledge is limited. Imagination encircles the world' (Viereck, 1929, p. 117).

1.8 billion of the world's population was between 10 and 24 year olds in 2014 (UNESCO, 2015), which means that even today, that number constitutes the young adults. Instead of mocking the millennials and taking potshots at the new generation, you may be well advised to understand and embrace them. This is your customer. If they don't like you, your businesses don't have too many years left. This generation has grown up in the creative era, where innovation has been almost a daily affair.

Businesses talk about innovation. They assume to understand and embrace it. Yet the 2020 pandemic exposed the cultural fabric of businesses—how not ready their cultures were to respond. A recent Indian retail market leader was acquired by a big conglomerate. One of my close associates asked the retail business entrepreneur about what his learning has been and why did he have to sell out. He replied, 'Don't surround yourself with mediocre people.'

Mediocrity is the comfort zone. It is accepting the status quo. It is the boardroom where what gets done is what the boss wants. It is uncreative. The data from the reports above tell us that success increasingly depends upon the ability to innovate. Creativity is central to the innovation and represents originality. Originality is the economic competitive advantage that all of strategic management so dearly professes.

Strategic thinkers, especially in large businesses and even so in entrepreneurial ventures, where entrepreneurs are out to impress the strategic investors, are reduced to being human calculators. They remind me of Excel sheets that somehow developed a voice. They forget that strategy itself is a creative process. The future doesn't exist. You create it. The future of business doesn't exist. You create it. Yes, planning has merit. But planning is simply guessing. Strategists, of course, aim to get the guessing game right.

So what do you do if you want to be accurate at something related to the future? You take the creativity out—and everything becomes perfectly predictable. No surprises! It also is the beginning of mediocrity. Businesses prefer to call it by different names—alignment, experience, business sense, etc.

Whatever be their terminology, one must remember that giants do fall. Consider the popular cases such as IBM losing the software business to Microsoft, Microsoft losing the Internet business to Google, Eastman Kodak losing out in resisting the digital wave, General Motors losing in the automobile industry and Kmart losing out in retail.

At the successful end of these stories are strategic innovations, and at the unsuccessful end of these are the experienced strategists.

APPLE FALLING SYNDROME

THE FLAW IN UNDERSTANDING CREATIVITY

An apple falls from a tree and leads to the revelations of Newtonian mysteries of gravitational forces. At another period in time, Apple becomes a path-breaking brand name owing to the creative madness of its founder.

When we look at creativity from the lenses of these exceptional achievements, it almost becomes an exception, rather than the norm. Then in our everyday experiences, we come across creative ideas that may seem out of sync and not rooted in realities. For example, some years ago I was witness to a meeting where a young enthusiast was explaining an unusual idea of a software development company to decision-makers. This company was in the business of front-end retail software solutions. The enthusiast poetically commented that his idea was 'on the edge of changing the way the world will buy'. The CEO, however, laughed and said, 'You're not on the edge, you're dangling in the clouds that have no edges.' Mobile payment solutions like the Apple Pay were launched in about 2014. I witnessed the idea being rejected in 2003.

'The creative types' is the usual adjective to describe someone who is a rebel, unreal or even frivolous. The reason is explicable; imagination may not always appear to be in sync with reality. In creative industries such as advertising, this is specifically true and even celebrated. Business has come to understand creativity in terms of ideas. This understanding is rooted in academic texts, much of which defines creativity as production of something novel and useful. Ideas are surely an outcome of creativity, but can creativity be defined in terms of ideas?

From the conception of a novel idea to its implementation, that is, when the world finally took notice, this period lasted for 17 years for Newton and, in the same manner, 15 years for mathematician Hamilton (Walia, 2019). To describe that as a stroke of luck or a moment of genius is mostly frivolous, as it overlooks the conscious process of creating and persevering to find an answer to a problem.

Our understanding of creativity is totally flawed. Creativity is not an idea and is certainly not a freak show like an apple falling from a tree.

Take the example of the classic Polaroid story (Berger, 2016). Back in the 1940s, Edwin Land was on vacation with his three-year-old daughter. He took a photograph of her, using a traditional film camera. The daughter wanted to see the results right away, not comprehending that the film must be sent off for processing. She asked, 'Why do we have to wait for the picture?' After hearing his daughter's why question, Land wondered if one could develop film inside the camera? He was stuck with the question then on how to bring the darkroom into the camera. That one 'why' question led to Land developing the Polaroid instant camera.

Apple became a brand not because it had unique ideas but because it solved problems.

We understand creativity as synonymous with creation. For example, if the end product is unique and useful, such as the iPod, then it must be creative. We don't understand the process of being creative and, hence, we find it more convenient to mock it. Imagine Newton describing the falling of an apple to a modern-day boardroom, 17 years before he was to explain it as gravity. It is highly likely that Newton may as well have been rendered jobless. Wasn't Steve Jobs shown the door at his own company?

Everyone is creative. If we weren't creative, then our lives would be perfectly predictable which they are not. As Land's Polaroid discovery shows us, creativity is a response to problem perception. The majority of us, whether it is businesses or people, don't perceive unique problems. We are overly obsessed with growth and numbers. Therefore, a differential response that doesn't fit into the world view of our problem is considered worthy of ridicule.

The digital camera was a laughable suggestion to the executives of Kodak, because their world view of the problem was how to make more money from the film camera.

The personal computer was a laughable proposition to IBM's executives because their world view was how to extract value from computers as a mainframe object.

The touch phone was laughable to most phone manufacturers because their world view was to exploit what they had created thus far.

What is laughable to your business? It just could turn out to be the event that threatens it the most.

Creative responses and innovations in an organization will be sought, implemented and judged, based on the problems that preoccupy it. Is your business occupied with unique problems or with majoritarian ones? That will decide how you behave creatively and how you judge creativity. And that decides the future of your success, because it is not that Newton was the first person who saw an apple falling. He happened to be the one who was preoccupied with a problem that others weren't.

GOOD IS NOT
THE ENEMY OF

GREAT

BINARY BLINKERS

Companies and entrepreneurs are constantly scanning opportunities. They must then exploit them for profit. Having invested resources to exploit an opportunity, a company unknowingly or purposely builds an expertise around it. Too much expertise tends to be anti creativity. Expertise is 'knowing' something rather too well, and creativity is venturing into the unknown. The conflict that faces most organizations is one between incremental and radical innovations. Should we make small improvements and continue to exploit or should we invest in radical changes and divest energies needed to exploit? This is a creator's dilemma.

When a horse runs on the race track, blinkers are used to black out all distractions but the race track. Expertise is a binary blinker of sorts. Having perfected the art and science of doing something, the expertise is too strong to see a possibility. Perhaps that's why they say that good is the enemy of great.

Apple and Amazon are great examples of ambidextrous companies that have managed both incremental and radical innovations to create sustained competitive advantages. Apple, for example, continues to improve its products such as the iPhone incrementally and yet works on radical disruptive innovations. Similarly, Amazon incrementally has added products to its storefront all the time and yet works upon radical innovations that are not its core business, such as Alexa, Prime Video or web services.

Creative potential as well as strategic potential for a company or an individual is a journey from what is to what can be.

Potential then is fundamentally an answer to three things:

1. Do I?

2. Can I?

3. Will I?

Do I see a possibility in imagination? Can I accomplish that possibility is a capability judgement that one makes not only on current capability but also future perceived capability. This would include the capability that a business or a person feels can be built or acquired. Will I pursue the opportunity is a matter of willingness, perseverance and belief to overcome the roadblocks.

The exploitative intent dominates the business world—the intent to get, acquire and amass with what exists within. The explorative intent, on the other hand, is the one to discover newer avenues and solve new problems. Someone has to be able to exploit to provide resources for another to be able to explore. Being good at exploitation need not be the enemy of being great. Yet very few companies on the planet are able to 'exploit' and 'explore'. They either exploit or explore. Remember the previous chapter about Mr O's brilliance. There was no brilliance in the 'or' situation, only in the 'and' situation.

Rising to a creative potential is not about expansion or investing resources in multiple avenues to create a bigger company. Creative potential begins with the problem that you see. The problem you currently solve must fund the problem that you will solve. If the problem you currently solve only funds exploitation of the same problem, then sooner or later that problem will become irrelevant because someone, somewhere in a garage will disrupt you.

An innovative organization will function somewhat like Figure 2.1.

An organization around expertise or exploitation will function somewhat like Figure 2.2.

As you can see, in a creative pursuit the problem will guide exploration, whereas in an exploitative pursuit the intent of exploitation itself will guide problem discovery.

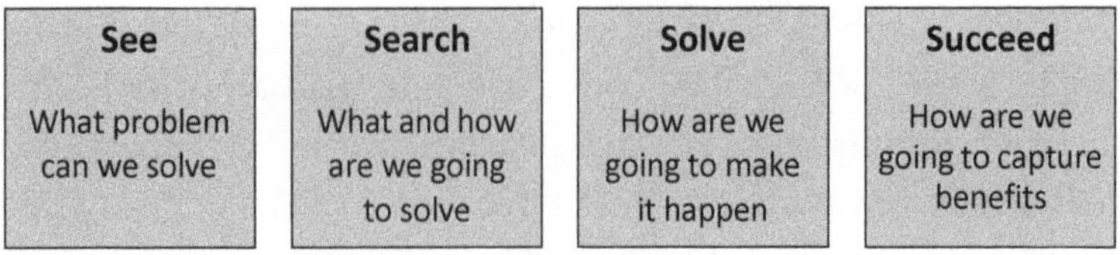

See	**Search**	**Solve**	**Succeed**
What problem can we solve	What and how are we going to solve	How are we going to make it happen	How are we going to capture benefits

Figure 2.1 The Innovative Process

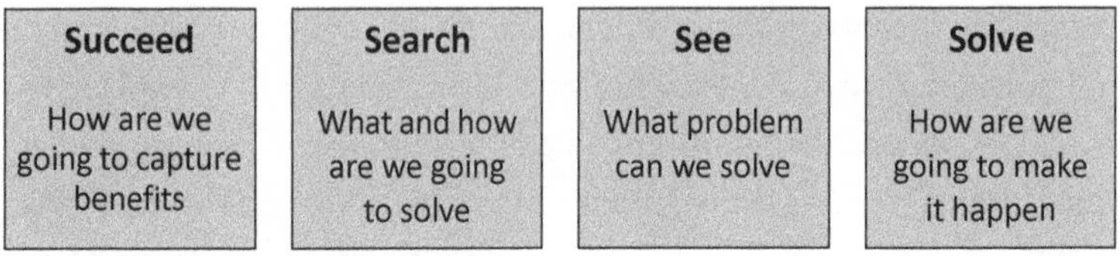

Succeed	**Search**	**See**	**Solve**
How are we going to capture benefits	What and how are we going to solve	What problem can we solve	How are we going to make it happen

Figure 2.2 The Reactive Process

MR B'S STORY

Years ago I heard Zig Ziglar, the motivational speaker, narrate a story. I am writing a version of it here.

Mr B called a meeting. He had all his people gathered together. He said, 'We've got a wonderful company, we are growing, we are expanding and things are going well. But some of us are becoming a little slack. Some come in a little bit late, some leave a little early and some spend too much time on coffee breaks and some too much over lunch. I recognize that some of it is my fault. I haven't set the kind of example I should have been setting. In the future, you can absolutely count on this. I am going to come in a little early and stay late. I am going to restrict all my personal phone calls, none I'll make. I am not going to do anything when I am on the job but just be on the job. I'll take shorter lunch breaks, shorter coffee breaks….' He really made the commitment. It was quite a speech. He set the example in place. He was very serious about it.

But you know, at times, in the excitement of things we make these speeches and then we forget about them. Well, that's what happened. About three weeks later, Mr B was at the country club for lunch and forgot about the time. All of a sudden he looked at his watch and said, 'Oh my goodness! I will now have to reach the office in about 10 minutes.'

In a moment, he hopped off the table, made a mad dash to the parking lot, jumped into his car, pressed on the accelerator and within 60 seconds from looking at his watch he was now racing at 100 km/s per hour. Left. Right. Zig. Zag. Tires burning. Unstoppable. But the long arm of the law entered the picture and gave him a ticket. Mr B was absolutely livid. He angrily said, 'This is absolutely ridiculous. Here I am, a peaceful taxpayer and a law-abiding citizen. All I was doing was going a little fast. I admit that. But you guys ought to be looking at the robbers and murderers and rapists and those bad guys disrupting peace. Leave us peace-loving people trying to uphold some values; leave us peaceful citizens alone.'

Mr B was really upset. By the time he got to office he was even more furious. He did what management has done, forever. Instead of calming down, he decided to shake the system a little more. In his loud voice, he called for the sales manager. And everybody in the office could hear him as he said, 'What I want to know is that did you close the deal on the ABC account?' The sales manager kind of ducked his head and said, 'Mr B I... I... I.... I don't know what happened on that deal. I thought I had it. It was all wrapped up. Signed, sealed and ready to roll. But at the last moment something happened and it came undone.'

Now, if you think Mr B was upset, you should have seen him now. He was raging mad. He shouted, 'This is ridiculous. You have been my sales manager here for 15 years and I have depended on you to get me business. And now, we had the chance to get the biggest business in the country, the biggest account of all and what do you do? You blow it. Well, let me tell you something, friend, just because you have been here for 15 years does not mean you have a lifetime contract. I want that business replaced. We needed that account to do the expansion that we needed to do and here you have lost the biggest opportunity we ever had. YOU replace that business or I am going to replace you.'

Oh! He was upset. But if you think he was upset, you should have seen the sales manager. He went storming out of B's office. He slammed the door behind his back. Muttering under his teeth, he said, 'This is ridiculous. For 15 years I have been the one to bring in all the business. If it hadn't been for me, this company would have gone down the drain years and years ago. And now, just because I miss one lousy sale, he uses the cheap trick. He threatens to fire me. This is not fair at all.' He called his secretary and said, 'You know that five letters I gave you this morning, have you got them out or have you been fooling around doing something else, making excuses about not getting your job done?' She said, 'No, don't you remember, you said that the XYZ account takes priority over everything else and that's what I have been working on.' The manager got wilder, 'Don't give me any lousy excuses. I said I want those letters out and I am going to tell you right now, if you can't get them out, I'll find someone who can. Just because you have been here seven years, that does not mean I'll give you a lifetime contract.'

Oh dear, he was really upset, but if you think he was upset, you should have seen that secretary. She went storming out of his office. She screamed to herself, 'This is ridiculous. For seven years I have been running this company. If it weren't for me, this company would have gone down the drain years and years ago. And now just because I can't do two things at once, he uses a cheap lousy trick and threatens to fire me. Him firing me, yeah right, as much as I know about him, who is he kidding?' She was really upset. She walked over to the receptionist. She sternly said, 'I have these five letters and I want you to get them out. Now. I know ordinarily this is not your job, but you are not doing anything anyhow, except for just sitting under the air conditioner out here and occasionally answering the phone.' Raising her voice further, she said, 'I want these letters out and if you can't do it, I'll get somebody who can. Don't for a moment think that you have a lifetime contract here.'

Oh dear, she was really upset, but if you think she was upset, you should have seen the receptionist. She cursed to herself, 'They don't do anything in this office anyway, except for gossip, talking, coffee and talking on the telephone. Every once in a while, they get a little bit of work out, and the minute they get behind, they come here and put it on my desk. Each one of them. And they say now you get this out. Hell, I am the only one who does anything out here. If not for me, this company would have gone down the drain years and years ago.' Oh, she was really upset, but she got the letters out. She got home. She was still furious. She walked in the front door. First thing she saw was her son lying down on the floor watching television. Second thing she saw was that he was still wearing his school uniform. The shirt was torn and had food marks all over it. She yelled, 'Son, how many time have I got to tell you that when you come back from school, put your play clothes on? Your mother has a hard enough time that she is working and sending you through to school. Now because you have been shamelessly disobedient, go upstairs right now. No evening meal for you and no television for the next three weeks.'

Oh dear, she was really upset, but if you think she was upset, you should have seen the little boy. He hopped; running upstairs, he said, 'This is ridiculous. I was doing something for my own mother. She doesn't even give me a chance to explain. Not fair.' He yelled, 'I don't like this house.' And about that time, listening to the loud voice, his little dog walked right in front of him. What a mistake!

The boy reached out and gave the little dog a big old-fashioned kick. And said, 'Now, you get out of here. You probably haven't done any good yourself.'

WOW.

You see our behaviours or ideas and actions about what to do almost impulsively follow emotions. Attitudes or situations dictate emotions. Core intents or beliefs dictate attitudes; for example, in all these people associated with Mr B, the core intent was to stay relevant. That determined the loss of relevance in the moments of ridicule. That determined the emotions of frustration and anger. And that determined the ideas and actions on how to deal with the next person almost instinctively.

Ideas will flow wherever intent goes.

REALLY

WHO WINS?

STRATEGIC INTENT AND CREATIVE OUTCOMES

Mr B's story is what characterizes negative value creation. Everyone feels that they won, and yet the summation of value is non-existent.

Strategic focus in companies today fundamentally lacks problem perception. The focus is driven by ambition, goals and the intent to maximize self-interest or gain. In a way, these are capitalistic notions. But do they work out?

Ambition is essentially outdoing the resources available to you. That establishes intent. The intent guides decisions and strategies. It also guides the problem we attempt to solve. In most cases, the problem turns out to be the gap in our ambitions and realities. Is that a real problem or a manifested one?

Companies such as Coca-Cola, Diageo, Kraft, Mars, Nestlé, PepsiCo, Philp Morris, SABMiller and Unilever are market leaders named in a report that says that they are manufacturing and distributing products that are the leading causes of deaths and diseases (Moodie et al., 2013). There are known health defects caused by the consumption of the products that are manufactured or distributed by these companies and have been termed as 'industrial epidemics'. Some of these companies have been identified as the leading causes of non-communicable diseases (NCDs), at the 2011 UN high-level meeting on NCDs (Moodie et al., 2013). NCDs accounted for 63 per cent of 57 million global deaths in 2008 (World Health Organization, 2011, p. 1–176).

Now that is an example of negative societal value creation. Are these companies doing well? Of course, they are. Are they creating value? They are profitable for sure. The total value creation for all of the stakeholders created is debatable.

What problems are you solving?

Is it a unique problem, meaning, that if you don't solve it, does the problem remain unsolved?

And if not, why the hell are you doing what you're doing?

And if yes, then are you certain that the business is having a positive impact on total value creation?

Entrepreneurship is not about creating wealth alone. It becomes sustainable only when it solves a problem and creates value for everyone. Take, for example, the leading Indian company, Reliance Industries. It recently caused disruption in the telecom sector and rendered over 50 per cent of telecom companies to an almost bankrupt situation. However, the venture did so by solving a problem of penetration and pricing. Facebook solved a problem first. Uber solved a problem. Google solved a problem.

Creativity follows problem perception. Whether you are targeting solving a problem of your ambitions or an actual one, the ideas will flow. The danger is that the problems of ambitions usually lead to a negative creation.

My team recently did an academic empirical experiment to study the correlation between intents and creative outcomes (Walia, in press). We got the top decision-makers of four leading global companies to participate in the study. The results were a revelation.

The analysis of the study found that the primary intents of maximizing profits, that is, a business guided by the prime goal of making money, had the most negative effect of value creation. They engaged in practices, decisions and outcomes that were unethical and produced damaging results. The primary intent of securing a competitive advantage for themselves fared slightly better but had a neutral impact on value creation. That is, the advantage rotated between different players at different times, making no impact on total value creation. It was the primary intent of discovering unsolved problems that have the most positive and upward impact on total value creation.

Think back to Mr B's story in the previous section. It is almost as if it may have been far better that Mr B spared all those people and went and kicked the dog straight away by himself. Everyone got their share of revenge in the story and yet no one won. They all lost something.

Creativity always meets strategy. The question is whether it meets it positively or negatively. The answer lies in the strategic intent. Do you exist to solve a problem or to create them?

CREATION

IS PAINFUL

NOT A BAG OF TRICKS

So what is creativity?

How does a business view creativity?

And how does a creative or innovative product come about?

The most common understanding of creativity is that it involves the production of something novel or original and useful. Our understanding of creativity stems from judging the end product. The process of producing the creative thing is largely unobservable.

We see an iPod or Tesla automobile or a new platform in the social space and conclude if that is innovative or not. Simply, the question is: Is that novel and useful?

But how do the sparks of imagination get triggered in the brains of people who go about creating these? What is being creative? The end product gives hardly any insight on how it came to be created.

Let us break down creativity into three separate but interlinked processes. First, there is the process of being creative. Then, there is the creation of the product. Lastly, there is the judgement of whether the creation is actually creative. The current understanding of creativity in business, basically, exists only at the third stage. Decision-makers play gatekeepers and pass judgements on viability.

Creativity—the process—is triggered by a perception of the problem. The individual's problem perception then triggers the productive activity in the brain. Productive activity (and not reproductive activity) is basically imagination. As was written earlier in the book, the process between this trigger to creation can be very long, as were the 17 years for Newton. The process goes through formulations, corrections, calibrations, trials and misses and, finally, may or may not become a creation. Once it does lead to creation, it interacts with gatekeepers or decision-makers regardless of the field you work in. They are decision-makers in our companies, publishers in academia, producers or directors in films, or the parliament in politics. The gatekeepers decide the utility and whether or not to introduce it to the world.

Take a look at the following reactions. They are a reflection of how some of the most obvious outcomes, in hindsight, were dealt with by the decision-makers at initial stages (Schoemaker, 1995).

'Heavier-than-air flying machines are impossible.'
—Lord Kelvin, British Mathematician,
Physicist and President of the British Royal Society, c. 1895

'With over fifty foreign cars already on sale here the Japanese auto industry isn't likely to carve out a big slice of U.S. market for itself.'
—Business Week, 2 August 1968

'A severe depression like that of 1920–1921 is outside the range of probability.'
—The Harvard Economic Society,
16 November 1929

'I think there is a world market for about five computers.'
—Thomas J. Watson, Chairman of IBM, 1943

'There is no reason for any individual to have a computer in their home.'
—Ken Olison, President, Digital Equipment
Corporation, 1977

'We don't like their sound. Group of guitars are on the way out.'
—Decca Recording Co. Executive,
turning down the Beatles in 1962

'The phonograph ... is not of commercial value....'

—Thomas Alva Edison, Inventor of
the Phonograph, c. 1980

We will deal with decision-making in Stage 4 of this book. However, for now, the reader must remember that creativity depends upon problem perception. It is not about some trick pulled out from air and then translated into a product. It is about a passionate dedication to solve a problem. Even before that, it is about discovering the problem itself. You don't have to do something in order to be creative. If a unique problem troubles you enough, your imagination kicks off, much like a child who cannot find an answer to a question.

I presented a question in the previous chapter, and I'll ask it again now: What is the unique problem that you are solving? If the problem perceived by you is not unique, that is, if someone else is already solving it, then you will always be fighting for pennies and bargains.

Strategic brilliance is like an outcome in itself, a creative outcome, the creative outcome of solving a unique problem, for which the critical skill needed is the sensitivity or ability to perceive a problem in the first place.

COME OUT OF OUTCOME THINKING

Creativity is a goal-directed activity. It follows the direction of intents. We now know that if the intents are to make profits or to be better than another, it really doesn't lead to any positive value creation.

As much as people will cognitively admit to understanding this, I think that psychologically people don't realize that profits and competitive advantages are mere outcomes. When they become directives and goals that surpass everything else, then the direction of creativity becomes subservient to that goal. Research has shown that within that limited scope, creativity either diminishes or turns deviant. The dot-com bust and subprime mortgage crisis are prime examples of these.

Value capture will follow value creation, but when value creation becomes a slave to value capture, one has lost their intelligence to derive problems in favour of greed.

Creative potential—a journey from what is to what can be—is not a journey from what I have to what I can have, but rather a journey from what value I provide to what value I can provide. Creativity begins with problem perception, so creative potential must begin with perceiving the problem. Maximizing potential is not about thinking in terms of getting the lion shares of the pie. That may as well be an outcome, but the route to it lies in solving a problem and not in comparisons. Businesses have to compete. That's the nature of our economies. Solving problems rather than competing on existing solutions automatically keeps one ahead.

Managements around the world have fallen into the paradigm of thinking and obsessing about outcomes. As a result, they strategize for that. In the process, they overlook discovering new problems. Outcome thinking is what happened to Donald Trump, the former president. The decisions he took followed the phrase 'putting America first' and ended up destroying the American dream itself.

Instead of strategizing and making a budget sheet for 'capturing value', the brilliant model will be to first prepare one for 'discovering unloved problems'.

REFERENCES

Barsh, J., Capozzi, M., & Mendonca, L. (2007, October). How companies approach innovation: A McKinsey global survey. *The McKinsey Quarterly.* https://www.elkarbide.com/sites/default/files/MCKINSEY%20INNOVACI%C3%93N.pdf

Berger, W. (2016). *A more beautiful question: The power of inquiry to spark beautiful ideas.* Bloomsbury.

Dawson, P., & Andriopoulos, C. (2017). *Managing change, creativity and innovation.* 3rd ed. SAGE Publications.

Schoemaker, P. J. H. (1995). Scenario planning: A tool for strategic thinking. *Sloan Management Review, 36,* 25–40.

UNESCO. (2015). *Cultural times: The first global map of cultural and creative industries.* EYGM Limited.

Viereck, G. S. (1929). What life means to Einstein: An interview by George Sylvester Viereck. *The Saturday Evening Post,* p. 117.

Walia, C. (2019). A dynamic definition of creativity. *Creativity Research Journal, 31*(3), 237–247.

Walia, C. (2021). Creative–strategic theoretical model: Conclusions and implications. In *Creativity and Strategy.* Springer Nature.

Moodie, R., Stuckler, D., Monteiro, C., Sheorn, N., Neal, B., Thamarangsi, T., Lincoln, P., & Casswell, S. (2013). Profits and pandemics: Prevention of harmful effects of tobacco, alcohol, and ultra-processed food and drink industries. *The Lancet, 381,* 670–679.

World Health Organization. (2011). *Global status report on non-communicable diseases 2010.* Italy.

STAGE THREE

DO YOU HAVE A PROBLEM?

ROOTS OF
OUR ECONOMIC THOUGHTS

CAPITALISM AND I

Adam Smith, often regarded as the grandfather of capitalist thought, concluded the following:

> It is not from the benevolence of the butcher, the brewer, or the baker that we expect our dinner, but from their regard to their own interest. We address ourselves, not to their humanity, but to their self-love, and never talk to them of our own necessities, but of their advantages. (Schwartz, 1992; Smith, [1776] 1976)

Capitalism is understood as an ideology where the society has an opportunity to get what it wants (profits, wages or products) within a competitive market, where each one pursues self-interest. Such competition is supposed to drive quality upwards and prices downwards and, therefore, benefit the society. This ideology encourages the pursuit of self-interest amid competition and engenders a 'winner-take-all' mindset. For example, the richest 1 per cent of Americans own 40 per cent of the country's wealth, while the bottom 80 percent own only 7 percent (George, 2014).

Nevertheless, capitalism has many strong points: Technological advancements, provision of valuable goods and services, newer and more effective means of communication, simplification of access to travel and medical treatments and advancements lead many to conclude that capitalism is the only way to successfully organize the economic life and that 'there is no alternative' (TINA; Kasser et al., 2007).

More recently, ideas such as 'sustainability, social responsibility, shared value creation and responsible innovation' have been developed to guide capitalism into a well-meaning direction. The need to add 'responsible' in front of innovation or 'shared' in front of value creation is all too revealing, isn't it?

BP went from being regarded the 'greenest' energy company to one of the most environmentally destructive ones in less than a decade (O'Toole & Vogel, 2011). Apple, driven by maximizing profit per employee, contracted over 700,000 workers in Asia and Europe, resulting in huge employee layoffs; 636,484 employees were laid off in the USA between January and May 2012 (George, 2014). The working conditions at the Chinese Foxconn factory, where iPads are manufactured, have been highly questionable; an explosion in 2011 killed and injured workers, and suicide attempts were reported in the workers' dormitories (Duhigg & Bradsher, 2012). Fifty-two of the largest 100 economies are corporations (i.e., 52 corporations' economic activity is greater than that of most nations; Mander et al., 2001)—a sign of great success and proof that companies and entrepreneurs do succeed in maximizing self-gains. Around 70 per cent of these leaders, across a range of industries, believe that keeping innovation among their top three priorities helps them drive growth. When entrepreneurial leadership combines with innovation, the leaders almost enjoy a heroic status. Leaders like Indra Nooyi (PepsiCo), Tim Cook (Apple) and Mark Zuckerberg (Facebook) are often treated like celebrities.

Capitalism has encouraged values and beliefs that people can achieve anything through hard work, individualism and even greed. Legal systems, governments, stock markets, media, trade organizations and other institutions form the system that supports this ideology. That is the way the world understands and appreciates progress. Research has demonstrated that the need for achievement and power are the prime goals for capitalism, and these are psychologically opposed to thinking universally and holistically (Kasser et al., 2007).

This book is not judging whether capitalism is good or bad, but merely pointing out that the root of our economic thought process is centred in 'I', in the self-interest. The economic thought process drives much of our ambitions, goals, lives and societies. It also drives the way we perceive problems and solutions, or innovations. It, therefore, drives our companies and strategies. But the very companies and strategies of the most celebrated leaders are also driving NCDs (as mentioned before), unethical practices, privacy legislations, climate changes, social unrest and even political manipulations.

Certainly, the 'I' factor can be considered as progress, but can it be considered as brilliant?

NOT ON THE
SHOULDERS
OF GIANTS

DARK SIDE OF INNOVATION

There is an inherent belief that innovation is good. Of course, innovation is essential in business and in life. Innovation, though, is neither good nor bad. It is driven by intent. It can produce both positive and negative outcomes.

The case of 9/11 is often used to describe negative innovations in academic literature. The perpetrators of 9/11, for example, came up with a highly innovative idea to fly planes into the twin towers. From the perspective of the terrorists, it was novel and useful. In most empirical checklists for innovation, the act would tick off as a valid innovation study. Interestingly, unlike in business, this particular dark act can be attributed to a perpetrator for fixing responsibility.

The dark side of innovation surrounds us. Companies producing products that are responsible for spreading disease, destruction of the environment, addictive substances, harm from radiations produced by technology, privacy invasions, political interferences, corporate crimes, banking scandals and corruption are all evident and prevalent. The problem, unlike the 9/11 case, is that no one is really responsible for it. This is called indeterminable responsibility. That is when the harm is produced but the structures are so complex that it is not attributable to any specific person or company or agent and, therefore, remains legal.

This is the 'I' factor in action and an absence of a universal understanding or intelligence. The dominating economics, though is a process operating in highly competitive scenarios, establishes intent within us that knowingly or unknowingly produces acts of deviances. The result is that in that moment of producing a dark innovation, we might be better off individually, but as whole everyone pays a price.

Put the laws of economics aside for a moment. The laws of nature are very clear—'as you sow so shall you reap'. Fundamentally, dark innovations are unsustainable. Firms usually get away because of indeterminable responsibility. However, the dark side can prove to be an existential threat. For example, the estimated costs from legal proceedings against firms cost over $30 billion for Volkswagen and over $61 billion for BP (Schwartz & Bryan, 2017).

Leaders and decision-makers within companies probably don't even, for a moment, feel that something wrong is about to happen or is happening. It is business as usual to see a problem, formulate a strategy, act and produce results. If the results happen to trigger something negative, there is always a legal department and a PR firm to convince the world that it was indeed good for them. After all, the very same firms run social programmes, schools, charities and, in some parts of the world, even religious institutions.

Our understanding of what the problem is determines the direction of creativity and innovation. When the intent itself is to beat the other side or to maximize the 'I' factor, imagination triggers it in that direction, without differentiating between good and bad.

Life is not a soccer match.

Business is not a soccer match.

You can't press a button on the remote, gossip about it in a pub and pretend it never happened. The consequences linger on. Cultures get shaped. Societies get impacted. Beliefs get perpetuated.

The 'I' factor is the dark side of innovation. It does no good to add the word responsible in front of innovation or create a social drive.

Self-interest is fine. No one is suggesting to not create wealth, jobs, technological advancements and alike. By all means do. Just be aware that within this mindset of operating and discovering problems from the 'I' factor, the probability of you operating in the dark side is significantly greater.

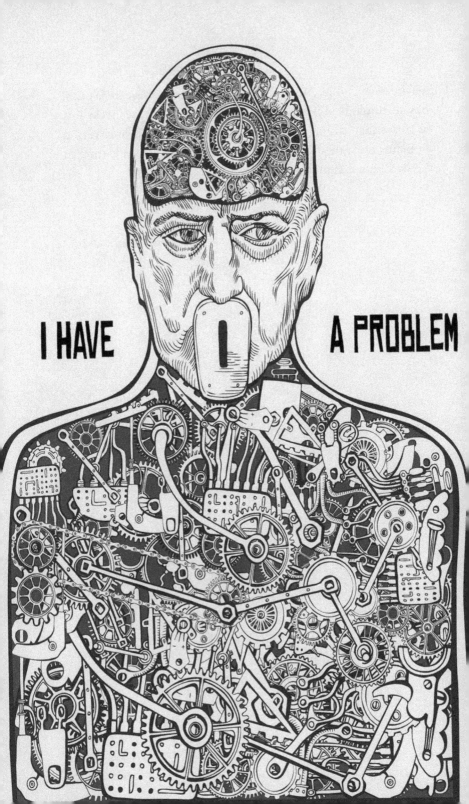

YOUR PROBLEM IS NOT EVEN A PROBLEM

What determines the strategic direction of a company?

A business has goals, targets or ambitions. It goes about its operations. It produces results. The results often fall short of the ambitions.

There it is—we have a problem!

Or

The results exceed expectations. Now we have a greater ambition. The results must now exceed the new ambition.

There it is—we have a problem!

A problem is typically understood as gaps between aspirations and current realities or results. Theoretically, problems are deviations from acceptable conditions that result in symptoms that need to be addressed. Businesses and individuals typically formulate their problems based on performance feedback. One's ambitions and aspirations, therefore, are the keys to triggering a problem search. This happens usually in three directions. A comparison between goals and reality, between the past and current performance or a social comparison with another as a benchmark. Poor performance or dissatisfaction with performance is a necessity for a problem to exist in our lives and in our businesses (Posen et al., 2018).

Having identified the problem, the business goes about framing it, searching for solutions, implementing the solutions and capturing value from the solutions. The captured value presents the next gap, and the cycle goes on.

The whole process of problem identification in established companies, particularly, is a process of politicking, polarization between different stakeholders, group biases, personal payoffs and precedence. Within these realities, the search for a problem tends to be within one's knowledge framework or expertise and is aimed excessively at the potential of the exploitation of the problem.

The problem is, of course, solved once the gap disappears.

The gap can also disappear by lowering the ambition itself.

So was your problem really a problem?

Is aspiration the problem that a business is trying to solve?

Or is there an actual problem that you perceive needs to be solved?

Unfortunately, management education and expertise development has conditioned us to view problems much like a mathematical exercise. In mathematical formulations, there will be a single correct answer. However, in an actual problem, the answer is a reflection of the way the problem is perceived. If we perceive problems as a gap between ambitions and realities, then the solutions will be sought for that. But is that a problem?

Companies talk about being purpose and mission driven. I have often read purpose statements in organizations and asked business leaders, 'What problem is your purpose solving?' The most established of organizations are often dumbfounded at that question. The reason is simple. They don't know.

People and organizations talk about being or wanting to be purpose driven and even discover a life purpose.

You have a purpose or your business has a purpose if and only if it is solving a real problem; else it is totally dispensable by the society, government, nation, industry and customers.

Before we move on, let me ask you the same question: What problem are you solving, can solve or will solve, which is not driven by your ambition but by your concern? Is that problem unique? Or, in other words, does your intervention really matter?

This determines the direction of your creative thinking and the utility of it.

DIME
PARADIGM SHIFT

PROBLEM PERCEPTION IS BRILLIANCE

Readers may hear of the KISS acronym, 'keep it simple, stupid'. In understanding strategic brilliance, it may well be replaced with the PISS acronym, 'problem is the solution, stupid'.

I interact with a whole lot of academicians and researchers. One of the academicians I met at an academic conference on creativity happened to be a Nobel Prize-winning physicist. He told me that you know you are on track to win a Nobel Prize when you present your research and it is so evidently embarrassing that every other physicist in the room has a certain dumb look on their face that says, 'Oh shit! Why didn't I think of that?'

Problems are everywhere. Let me give you a few examples that you will find are widely published in the World Health Organization and United Nations websites.

Human race survives on 0.05 per cent of the world's water. It adversely affects 2 billion people.

Worldwide, 2.36 million healthcare workers and 1.9 million managerial and support positions are needed. One billion people worldwide have no access to healthcare.

Because of unavailability of surgeons, 143 million People die in a year.

There is global teacher shortage of 18 million, and 23 per cent of the people have no access to education.

Annually, 70 million people are displaced as a result of war. One in every 113 people globally is now a refugee, an asylum-seeker or internally displaced. 16.6 per cent of the population have a sleep disorder. One billion people have food shortage. 2.3 billion people suffer from obesity.

Any solution to these problems represents a dramatic social change but that aside, it also represents a dramatic business opportunity.

The symptoms, signs and effects of every single one of these problems are visible in your neighbourhood. We just do not see them.

Why?

Because our economic thought process limits our ability to perceive problems independent of us.

Problem perception is purpose. Whether that perception for you is a gap between aspiration and results, or whether it is a real problem to solve.

Problem perception drives creativity, innovation and strategic direction. It is the outcome of your intelligence.

Your problem perception drives your brilliance or the lack of it. Einstein, Edison, Ford, Disney, Jobs, Gates, Gandhi, Martin Luther King, Mandela or Teresa were not students who were considered intelligent in their educational institutions. They were all creators though. They solved problems because they could see them, not because they topped in a business school.

Discovering a problem is as critical to innovation as innovation in itself is. In fact, problem discovery in itself must be considered a creative act. That is, can you discover a problem that is unique and useful in itself? If you do, then you have a purpose-driven business. If you don't, then you are welcome to the 'me too' club and can, at best, hope to enjoy the Red Queen's race.

PROBLEM MYOPIA

In 1969, Eric Hobsbawm noted that the goals of the firm supersede its creative and innovative intent:

It is often assumed that an economy of private enterprise has an automatic bias towards innovation, but this is not so. It has a bias only towards profit.

The goal of strategy within businesses is to create competitive advantage and, ultimately, profit. As we were discussing earlier, these itself result in problem identification. This is exactly what problem myopia is.

Problem myopia is defined as the inability to perceive a problem independent of strategic aspirations, for example, competitive advantage. Problem myopia is the predominant 'I' factor. It limits and directs the situational triggers for our imagination and, therefore, even limits the creative potential.

How do you move from problem myopia to problem perception? It's simple really. You see beyond yourself as your prime interest. When you do, problems are no longer the gap between your ambitions and results.

Let us define a problem beyond the academic roots and understand it for what it actually is.

A problem is to perceive different and interrelated environments to discover and bring disequilibria therein into one's intelligence. That is, a problem is to understand and acknowledge suffering. In perceiving different environments and sufferings therein, different stakeholders and their expectations are likely to emerge. There may be no correct answers or interpretations available initially, as like any creative process, the problem is also likely to evolve through exploration. The formulations may be conflicting to different interest groups and that is why it is a problem.

How might one then define the strategic problem in a strategic brilliance context? Here it is. A strategic problem is defined as an evolving, relevant and integrative articulation of the problem (derived from acknowledging disequilibrium in multiple inter-connected environments).

Conventional management approaches rely on feedback mechanisms to discover problems. Although performance feedback is crucial to identify gaps in efficiency, it does not provide any insights into the choice of problem or 'aspiration'. The detection or perception of significant and actual problems requires a change in the mindset to perceive problems not only as aspirations but also as they exist, which is independent of aspirations.

It is when the problems cannot be associated with the certainty of available solutions that you actually have a creative problem. This now allows for a purposeful direction. Of course, one may not succeed in solving this. However, you have entered the life of a true creator.

Take a look at a few creation examples and this will become clearer.

The iPad was developed in response to perceiving the problem that the world has inadequate teachers.

The automobile was conceived by Henry Ford because he didn't want horses to be on the roads, as they didn't belong there.

The Walmart strategy aimed at enabling the common man to be able to buy the same things as a rich man.

Walt Disney conceived the Disney Land post the Depression years as a tool to make people happy.

Much of Sony's strategy in the 1950s was to change the image around the world that 'Made in Japan' means something shoddy.

Google was conceived as a business plan in a business school as a project where its founders realized that information is not easily accessible.

Mark Zuckerberg was against opening advertisements in Facebook as his original plan was simply to connect people.

The current strategic mindset of problem identification is a strategy formulation approach to derive competitive advantage. While this may be leading to economic benefits for the firms, it may, in effect, be limiting the creative potential, as well as leading it to the dark side of innovations.

THE HERD
IS THE
UNCREATIVE
MAJORITY

THE STORY OF THE TINY FROG

There was once a group of tiny frogs who arranged a running competition. The goal was to reach the top of a very high tower. A big crowd gathered around the tower to see the race and cheer for the competition. The race began.

Honestly, no one in the crowd really believed that the tiny frogs would reach the top of the tower. They kept saying, 'Oh! Way too difficult. They will never make it to the top' and 'Not a chance; they will not succeed. It's too high.'

The tiny frogs began collapsing one by one, even while there were those who were climbing higher and higher. The crowd continued to yell, 'It's too difficult; no one will ever make it.' More tiny frogs got tired and gave up.

But one tiny frog continued higher and higher and higher. This one will just not give up! In the end, all the others had given up climbing the tower, except for this one tiny frog, who after a big effort was the only one to reach the top!

Then all the other tiny frogs naturally wanted to know how this one had managed to do it? One of the contestants asked the tiny frog who had won that how he had found the strength to reach the goal. The tiny frog did not answer. The winner was deaf.

Creative pursuits are not a majority thing. Majority opinions and advices are not going to be novel or original. Similarly, the problems majority associates with are going to be predictable and mostly shared. Problem perception in the way it is presented here is almost about breaking away from the majoritarian thoughts so that one is able to observe what it really is.

Interestingly, the tiny frog has a real-life parallel. Thomas Edison was totally deaf in one ear and hard of hearing in the other. His mother had to educate Edison at home. He had just days of professional schooling. By the time he died on 18 October 1931, Thomas Edison had amassed a record of 1,093 patents.

CREDO

BRILLIANCE CREDO

Get out of the 'I' mindset of what you hope to get and answer the following questions:

1. In your domain or environment, what disequilibrium can you observe?

2. Why do you think these are disequilibrium?

3. How are these currently being addressed by you or by someone else?

4. What are the gaps in the current solutions?

5. On a scale of 1–10, how much does this problem trouble you?

6. If your answer was less than 8, start over.

Without thinking of probable solutions, yet answer the following questions:

1. How would you frame the problem above in a single sentence?

2. What are the other incidental or supplementary problems that arise from this problem?

3. Is the problem saleable; that is, will enough people buy the problem in the manner that you have articulated it?

4. If not, then start again at number 7.

5. On a scale of 1–10, how committed do you feel to solve this problem?

6. If your answer was less than 10, start reading over again from Stage 3.

REFERENCES

Duhigg, C., & Bradsher, K. (2012, 22 January). For Apple, 'Made in USA' is a relic of bygone era. *Houston Chronicle*, A23, B28.

George, J. M. (2014). Compassion and capitalism: Implications for organizational studies. *Journal of Management*, 40(1), 5–15.

Kasser, T., Cohn, S., Kanner, A. D., & Ryan, R. M. (2007). Some costs of American corporate capitalism: A psychological exploration of value and goal conflicts. *Psychological Enquiry*, 18(1), 1–22.

Mander, J., Barker, D., & Korten, D. C. (2001). Does globalization help the poor? *International Forum on Globalization*, 1(3), 2–5.

O'Toole, J., & Vogel, D. (2011). Two and a half cheers for conscious capitalism. *California Management Review*, 53(3), 60–76.

Posen, H., Keil, T., Kim, S., & Meissner, F. (2018). Renewing research on problemistic search—a review and research agenda. *Academy of Management Annals*, 12(1), 208–251.

Schwartz, J., & Bryan, V. (2017, 29 September). VW's dieselgate bill hits $30 bln after another charge. Reuters. https://www.reuters.com/article/legal-uk-volkswagen-emissions-idUSKCN1C4271

Schwartz, S. H. (1992). Universals in the content and structure of values: Theory and empirical tests in 20 countries. In M. Zanna (Ed.), *Advances in experimental social psychology* (Vol. 25, pp. 1–65). Academic Press.

Smith, A. ([1776] 1976). *An inquiry into the nature and causes of the wealth of nations*. Random House.

STAGE FOUR

YOUR INTENT

Mediocre or Brilliant

DON'T RAISE THE BAR

THROW IT AWAY

RELATIONSHIP BETWEEN MEDIOCRITY AND EXCELLENCE

Change is a gradual, slow process. Nothing really changes overnight.

Too much creativity and innovation are rejected by the gatekeepers or decision-makers in any field. If you are an executive presenting an idea to a boardroom full of decision-makers, too much novelty is rejected. The reason is fairly obvious. Decision-makers need to protect what exists, ensure continuity and have predictability for acceptance of the idea. Overtly novel solutions will be unpredictable.

Take, for example, the smartphone. Smartphones didn't come about overnight. Mobile phones already existed. The palm pilot was a so-called 'touch device' that people were getting used to and touch phones were still being experimented by existing players. Apple then entered the market with their own version of a mobile phone. This was not overnight, just as the ouster of smartphone wouldn't be.

Businesses and people innovate. They come up with newer innovations and redefine the competitive landscape. Gradually, the bar raises for everyone else. They either catch up or fall by. By the virtue of progress, yesterday's excellence becomes today's mediocrity. This is true for business and for people and their skills. Unfortunately, we rarely look at our skill sets in that manner.

Companies keep talking about raising the bar. The innuendo is borrowed, of course, from the high jump analogy. What companies mean by raising the bar is to have higher ambitions and targets. In a high jump, the bar is the target. The bar is the jumper's operative method, so to say. It helps the jumper to focus. In business, the bar represents profits or revenues. That is an outcome of the operation. When it becomes the central focus, as we have discussed before, the value creation recedes. Companies tend to be operationally efficient but strategically inefficient. That is, they may have acquired expertise on managing their business but experience a complete dearth of creativity to generate novel strategic solutions for the future. Moreover, decision-makers resist novelty.

Our management education and business knowledge, in general, trains us to be excellent. It is oriented towards expertise, that is, being the best at something. Too much expertise is the antithesis to innovation.

An analysis of the top 100 firms in the Fortune 500 as of 1955 found that all of the firms barring one either made or handled physical things. A comparative of that with the corresponding Fortune 500 list of 2012 indicated that only 39 of the top 100 were involved in making things (McGrath & Kim, 2015). Retailers like Walmart and financial services like Citigroup have replaced the manufacturers. Even the manufacturers on the list were high-technology companies such as Apple, Google and Cisco. The 1955 companies didn't evolve. They remained excellent in their core skills. Their skills became mediocre over time because someone else innovated.

Everyone strives for excellence. Excellence is not unique. It is almost a benchmark, like the bar. Yes, it is needed. It is needed to solve problems, to function the wheels of the business and society. Yet it is tomorrow's mediocrity.

This is the problem with 'raise the bar' thinking—it is still a limitation. It is about getting better with yesterday's knowledge. It is about improving what exists. It is about waiting for the expertise to become mediocre and hoping that no one else is good enough to let that happen.

Throw the bar away. You are not a high jumper. Business is not an Olympic sport that happens every four years. Rather, four years are enough to wipe out generations of business's successes. Excellence and mediocrity are two sides of the same coin. Excellence is best served when it combines with innovation. It is not about choosing excellence instead of innovation. Brilliance itself is excellence and innovation.

Decision-makers typically reject too much of innovation in favour of the predictability of expertise. It stems from wanting to protect yesterday's bar. While it works to offer continuity to a business, it eventually becomes the reason for its fall as well.

142-year-old legacy of Woolworth and 208-year-old legacy of Debenhams are the most recent examples. Add to that list the likes of Pan Am, Toys R Us, Compaq, Arthur Anderson, Enron— you have a full list of world-beating expertise that kept fighting to raise a bar that just didn't exist anymore.

IT WILL FALL

IT'S NATURE

OBSESSIVE LEGACY DISORDER

Human beings have tremendous anxiety with endings. We want things forever. Continuity is preferred over change. This can be observed in our relationships, places where we stay, houses that we build, streams that we specialize in and, of course, in businesses that we run. Yet an ending is the beginning of change. And businesses talk about creating openness to change and innovation.

Our obsession for significance and relevance for leaving a legacy after the ending of a career or life are disorders that probably become the reason that a majority doesn't have a legacy. People stay in toxic relationships, make suboptimal career choices to stay in a particular city, sacrifice risk-taking ability to pay their home loans, get stuck with specialist domains for the fear of starting over and some of this behaviour spills over in business where the popular saying goes 'to grow or die'.

There is no sustainable competitive advantage available to any business. It is mostly temporary. Other firms catch up. Strategy eventually decays. Innovation is, therefore, considered as an antidote to strategy decay, and continuous innovation is considered essential for reinventing competitive advantages as and when they erode.

A great deal of business energy gets invested in preventing the erosion or in preventing the legacy. The reality is that nothing is forever. This is not to say that businesses must not strive for longevity. They should. Longevity is not a sign of success, even though it may be considered to be so. The threat of non-continuance results in adopting the 'raise the bar' goals and shifts the focus from discovering new problems to solve to exploiting what is already available. Very soon people forget that the legacy is in solving problems, not in getting returns. As long as a business is solving newer problems, relevance is not threatened. It is, in fact, threatened when the problems being solved have become redundant. Some new-age companies like Apple have strategies to disrupt their own products to avoid falling into the legacy trap. Who would imagine that a company would kill the very iPod that revived it from the clutches of a shutdown to becoming a trillion-dollar company?

Do Wright brothers have a legacy?

Does George Eastman have a legacy?

Does Frank Woolworth have a legacy?

Does Steve Jobs have a legacy?

Does Dhirubhai Ambani have a legacy?

Regardless of what happened or happens to their company's legacy, it is what remains when you have solved a problem. Period. On the other hand, a legacy disorder is when one tries to prolong value capture in the hope of leaving a legacy. A research by a private consulting company claims that only 3 per cent of family businesses[1] survive into the fourth generation. That is the legacy disorder where business loses the 'creation' edge of the founders and worries about profits and revenues alone. This is as true for life as it is for business. Prolonging of a relationship, for example, is not a proof that it is adding value.

Every single company on the planet will eventually die, be taken over or replaced by another. There shall be no permanent legacy in continuance. The only legacy a business and a person may hope to leave is to solve a problem and then solve some more. Rest is economic reality that even economists don't manage to get right.

---

[1] http://sponsored.bostonglobe.com/rocklandtrust/more-than-8-out-of-10-family-businesses-have-no-succession-plans/

WHAT DO BRILLIANT MINDS DO DIFFERENTLY?

The symptomatic effect of obsessive legacy disorder is that business leaders have become chief XLS officers. The calculator has become the decision-maker. Whether or not a business will solve a problem is not about ability but about viability. Brilliance is available abundantly but whether or not it will be used depends not upon availability but upon whether the Excel sheet can prove feasibility.

An article published in a leading academic journal analysed 91 strategy definitions between 1962 and 2008 (Ronda-Pupo & Guerras-Martin, 2012). Another analysis of strategy management definitions took a 20-year perspective and presented a list of distinctive words that represent the definitional elements related to the field of strategic management (Nag et al., 2007). Neither of these analysis have the word 'problem' in any of strategic definitions. That is problem myopia.

Yet another study into the minds of geniuses such as Nash, Poincaré and Einstein reveals that these minds considered their greatest discoveries to be in times where their logical thought processes were not interfering with their perceptions about reality (Carson, 2014). The research on the study of geniuses has suggested that problem perception is the prime trigger of productive activity, and that has the potential to transform humanity (Feist, 2014).

Counting upon the empirical information available to us and on experience of having interacted with various companies and their leaders, here is what the brilliant minds do differently than the rest.

- They obsess over the problems they perceive and over the solutions to those problems. They don't obsess over the opportunities that those solutions would land in their bank accounts.

- Their passions towards their actions are born out of acknowledging the suffering that the problems may be causing. It is not born out of greed for accumulation.

- Their actions and activities are almost always domain specific. For example, whether it is Einstein, Jobs or Ford, the problem perceived could be anything, but the action is within a domain.

- The language of success and failure is mostly absent. The endeavour is to solve problems and create solutions. Success appears much later, if at all, and is not a driving factor. Passion is. Steve Jobs was thrown out of his own company. Edison invested a disproportionate amount of his earning in an attempt to create the candescent lamp. John Nash wouldn't be acknowledged for all his hardships until almost in the twilight of his life when he received a Noble Prize.

- Perseverance is not even optional. It is a way of life in creative pursuit. Innovative ideas do not succeed in the first attempt and may not even in the hundredth. The problem remains an important one to solve. The Wright brothers' first flight was only 12 seconds and covered 120 feet. The extraordinary success followed, but before that was all sweat and toil.

- Brilliance is an outward reality, and only in hindsight. What drives the mind is insights. What others see as brilliance is an outcome of seriously developed insights.

- The brilliant minds are generous teachers. This is out of experience. The best of the brilliant minds that I have come across have all been very generous teachers in sharing what they know. This is quite opposite to business realities who believe they must hoard knowledge for it to be valuable.

- Effectiveness over efficiency. One can do the wrong thing precisely and accurately. Brilliant minds are self-critical and open to feedback, so that they can do the right thing and not the acceptable one.

- They work hard because they aren't even aware of it. They lose sense of time while at it.

- They are okay and probably more at ease in not being popular or famous.

WOULDN'T EVERYONE FIND THE ROAD

IF THERE WERE ONE

THE BRILLIANT CO. LTD

Brilliance is an event that occurs as a result of an attempt to create. This usually is not a recurring act. For example, most Nobel Prize winners hardly ever create anything that noteworthy after having won the recognition. Only four laureates have ever won the Noble Prize again[2]. Creation is an individual(s)-led process. It takes energy. It takes time. It has its burnout. Creators probably do not stop creating in their own ways, but their motivations may change over time. In any case, an act of brilliance was not intended to be so but intended to solve a problem. Brilliance was a judgement by others, thereafter. More often than not, one would find that people who are considered brilliant by us would struggle to inform about the process they followed. This is because they wouldn't know. I happened to coach a brilliant creator who is currently leading one of the most successful IT companies. When I asked the gentleman about how he created what he did. He answered, 'I just kept filling the gaps.'

Is there a brilliant company, then? The answer is both yes and no. Brilliant companies do exist as they may be producing brilliance, but they may not do so forever. However, there are lessons to be learnt from such companies. *Harvard Business Review* produced a list of top-20 transformative companies in the last decade (Anthony et al., 2019). These were companies such as Netflix, Adobe, Amazon, Tencent, Microsoft, and Alibaba. The companies are considered transformative when:

- Their share of revenue from their new growth was significantly greater than their share of revenues from their core business. This indicated strategic transformation.

---

[2] https://www.bbvaopenmind.com/en/science/leading-figures/the-magnificent-four-who-received-the-nobel-prize-twice/

- Their transformations had a significant impact on customers and the industry in the past decade. This indicated problem-solving.

- The financials of the company showed potential to sustain the transformations over the next decade. This indicated economic success.

The key to remain brilliant, therefore, is to keep fuelling the transformative journey. That is in continuing to identify newer problems to solve and solving them successfully. This is where it's theoretically perceivable for companies to remain brilliant over a sustained period of time, more so than individuals. In practice, however, very few companies do so because the leaders get stuck.

The study of transformative companies tells us that behaviourally these organizations have four significant characteristics:

1. The leaders tend to be driving brilliance or transformation, that is, setting the direction to be constantly solving newer problems.

2. The companies and their leaders are comfortable in letting go of the past. For example, Intuit sold off five business divisions, including one which was the original business of the company. Siemens had to take a call on a 140-year-old electric power business that generated in excess of $30 billion. As we discussed earlier, endings are essential for beginnings.

3. They leveraged their capabilities in industries and areas where they chose to be newer entrants. Fujifilm was in the same boat as Eastman Kodak. It invested heavily in medical imaging, leveraging existing chemical technology and the know-how that the firm used in photographic film, launching a full product line of diagnostic equipment for hospitals and other healthcare providers. At the time of the study,

18 per cent of Fujifilm's $22 billion in revenue came from healthcare.

4. They made innovation a strategic capability. These companies were able to ensure that innovation was not an isolated department but an institutionalized capability.

In the end, brilliance is a 10-letter word that is determined by another 10-letter word—leadership.

BRILLIANCE IS
HINDSIGHT

IT'S NOT 'CAN YOU?' IT'S 'WILL YOU?'

People who have achieved brilliance didn't really set out to be brilliant. No one can predict if their perceptions, efforts and subsequent creations will be, in fact, considered brilliant. Brilliance is a hindsight. Rather, most genius-level creations are, in fact, recognized much after the people who created them have passed on. People don't know if they can be Einsteins, but that doesn't stop them from scientific explorations. People don't know if they can be Bill Gates, but that doesn't stop them from becoming entrepreneurs.

Everyone is creative. In your daily lives you are creative. Anyone who has ever lied for anything has invented something that didn't exist.

Creativity follows the direction of problem perception. Most business ventures are rooted in becoming bigger. Creative ideas within those follow that direction. People respond to what occupies them. If conversations within a company occupy people to think of exploitation, rather than exploration, they respond in that manner.

When companies say that they don't have innovative capabilities, it simply implies that they are more concerned with maximizing their existing assets. There is nothing wrong with this, but this is not a capability issue. Capability follows intent.

Following the intent to create and be brilliant may or may not lead to being recognized as such, and that stops many from even attempting. It is easier to conclude that one doesn't have the capability than to admit their fear of failure.

The question is not ;can you?' The question really is 'will you?'

Will you acknowledge the problems and shortcomings that exist around you and do something about it or won't you? Will your business see the possibilities of creating greater value for your customers by innovating on the solutions available or won't it? Will you decide to let go of the past and create space for the future or won't you?

No one can guarantee that if you do, you will be the next rock star. That is not why you should do it either. The focus has to be on solving a problem. The rest may or may not happen.

I can guarantee you two things though. If you don't walk that path, you will not be a rock star. Whether or not you walk down that path, your company still will not live forever.

In the end, it is about what makes sense to you—to live brilliantly at the risk of living lesser or to live longer at the cost of being mediocre? There is always a price to pay. Again, it isn't 'can you' but 'will you'?

That answer defines life. It defines business. It defines you.

BRILLIANCE CREDO

1. Rewrite your problem statement from the previous stage.

2. What would be the reality if that problem were to be solved? How would it look for other people? What would they gain? How would they be better off? How would the world be better off?

3. How can you combine excellence and brilliance or expertise and creativity to solve this problem?

4. What price will you have to pay to walk this path? Will you?

5. Imagine for a moment that you could actually be the person to solve this problem. Write a positive statement of reality that occurs when you do solve it. Then write a statement as to how you will solve it. And finally write a statement on what that means for your life and for your business. This is your strategically brilliant intent.

REFERENCES

Anthony, S. D., Trotter, A., & Schwartz E. I. (2019). The top 20 business transformations of the last decade. *Harvard Business Review*, September. https://hbr.org/2019/09/the-top-20-business-transformations-of-the-last-decade

Carson, S. H. (2014). Cognitive disinhibition, creativity, and psychopathology. In D. K. Simonton (Ed.), *The Wiley handbook of genius*(pp. 98–221). Wiley-Blackwell.

Feist G. J. (2014). Psychometric studies of scientific talent and eminence. In D. K. Simonton (Ed.), *The Wiley handbook of genius* (pp. 62–86). John Wiley & Sons.

McGrath, R. G., & Kim, J. (2015). Innovation, strategy & hypercompetition. In M. Dodgson, D. M. Gann, & N. Phillips (Eds.), *The Oxford handbook of innovation management* (pp. 397–419). Oxford University Press.

Nag, R., Hambrick, D. C., & Chen, M.-J. (2007). What is strategic management, really? Inductive derivation of a consensus definition of the field. *Strategic Management Journal, 28*(9), 935–955.

Ronda-Pupo, G. A., & Guerras-Martin, L. Á. (2012). Dynamics of the evolution of the strategy concept 1962–2008: A co-word analysis. *Strategic Management Journal, 33*(2), 162–188.

CREATE VALUE FIRST

NO ONE CARES
ABOUT YOUR STRENGTHS

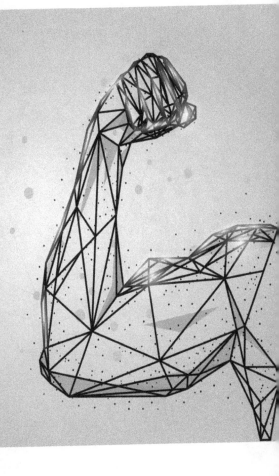

EXCELLENCE COMES WITH AN EXPIRY DATE

One of the hardest things to accept for people who are great at what they do is that they no longer will remain to be so. It is a classic case of denial and refusal to accept the loss of relevance.

In every field, knowledge is being created and updated all the time. The standards of excellence shift. Yesterday's excellence, even if iconic, loses relevance with changing times.

Michael Jackson, as iconic and excellent as he may have been, had one way to go—down.

Michael Schumacher was undoubtedly excellent but didn't remain the best, statistically speaking.

Kodak, perhaps, would still be excellent at film processing and related technologies, but who cares?

IBM built the advanced super computer, but ordinary and imperfect Microsoft machines were all that were ever needed to put it into an existential threat.

Wikipedia took out encyclopaedias.

Google Maps took out maps themselves.

Apple iTunes took out CDs and thumb drives.

Netflix is almost taking cable networks out.

Uber took out cab services.

Instagram took out photo albums.

Space X is plotting a commercial escape out of Earth.

A business may be excellent in conceiving and researching encyclopaedias, or be the best and most accurate creator of physical maps, or could produce the highest quality of compact discs, or may be the best content producer on cable television, or produce the best-looking photo albums, or, for that matter, be figuring out how Earth will accommodate green industrialization.

The fact is that no one cares what you are good at. The best of anything does not automatically add value today. A whole lot of established companies and even start-ups wait to have a perfect product ready before launching it. They fret over market sizes and calculations. They build crack teams. They secure business funding. Most established companies develop cold feet eventually, and most start-ups fail. They try to compete on excellence, and you surely can't better Michael Jackson if you are just about starting your career.

Can't better doesn't mean can't beat. An innocuous device with no changeable lenses, no printable quality, no multifunction modes, no flash light, no viewfinder, no lens cap, no multipurpose buttons and no ISO settings is the highest selling camera today, much in excess of the best that is available.

'What are you good at?'

'Stay true to your strengths.'

'Believe in what you do best.'

These time-tested, universal management jargons will lead to your demise. Period.

It doesn't matter what you are good at. It doesn't matter what your strengths are. It surely doesn't matter what you are best at. What matters is how you can combine different facets of what you have to create the value that no one does. That's it.

The value created doesn't have to be the best in the world. It has to be simply valued by those who will use it.

The gold medallists, the highest achievers or the best at something, is always a past tense statement. Most businesses, however, get trapped in competing with these standards and rarely match up. There are a few businesses who learn to ignore these standards and out-do the way they perceive value. These businesses end up becoming the future trends.

EXCELLENCE ISOLATES
BRILLIANCE COMBINES

GARAGE QUOTIENT

The reason why companies are often unable to create exponential growth models is that they confuse value creation with value capture. Capturing value is considered a proof for creating value. The focus then shifts to making money. That is a problem of isolation. As we have discussed previously, this, in effect, reduces the ability to create value.

Knowledge is never static. This is the simplest of insights that most businesses never come to terms with. Giant businesses are dusted to the ground, fighting new knowledge rather than embracing it. Why? Because their expertise is threatened if they accept that they have to learn something from the new kid on the block. Most firms, therefore, tend to build knowledge within their streams of expertise. Most individuals pursue knowledge acquisition within their own domains at best. This is almost suicidal.

Brooks Brothers probably were best at making tailored suits—shut down.

Hertz was probably the market expert for car rentals—filed for bankruptcy.

Virgin Atlantic built from experience—filed for Chapter 15 protection in New York.

Arthur Anderson was the equivalent of a Big Four consulting firm when it simply disappeared.

All of these companies and many more that have met similar fate do not really resist innovation. They innovate only within their expertise. They gather knowledge within their expertise. These are, in fact, the companies that became the best at what they do. They still have a customer base that would probably be loyal to their products. Their business strategies built around capturing value no longer work. Their knowledge base built around expertise can no longer compete with creating fresh value. It may be the lack of ability to capture value that may have shut them down, but it is the lack of creating value that have led to their intellectual bankruptcy before the actual one.

Figure 5.1 depicts a value creation matrix as an outcome of knowledge and innovation. Every firm or individual possesses knowledge and uses it to innovate to a certain extent. When the knowledge pursuit becomes limited combined with low innovative capability, the firm follows goals of efficiency. These will be cost-led strategies that are quite visible, for example, in the airline industry. When the pursuit of knowledge is high but

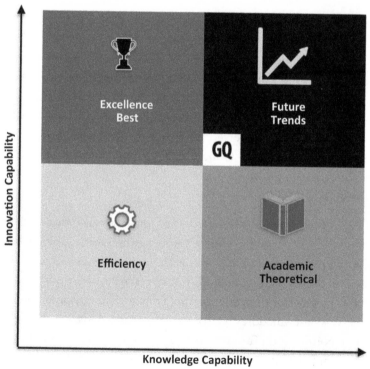

Figure 5.1 Garage Quotient

innovation is relatively moderate, it leads to a high level of academic expertise, for example, in the consulting companies. These companies tend to follow service model strategies, for example, the law firms.

When the knowledge remains moderate or specific to the domain and innovation is encouraged from within the firm's core areas, the firm tends to become excellent or the best in the world at its products or services. Such firms tend to follow premium pricing strategies, for example, automobile industry or the pharmaceutical industry. It is when the firms tend to follow a content knowledge expansion strategy with a constant innovation capability surge that they come in positions of defining future trends, for example Apple, Google and Amazon.

Value creation happens in all the four quadrants. Brilliance lies in combining new knowledge and innovation to create ahead of the curve. Even the smallest of these combinations represented by GQ or garage quotient is enough to end years of efficiency and excellence. Amazon, which started in a garage, was enough to threaten and virtually put an end to book stores. A business plan conceived in Stanford Graduate School of Business would create Google that virtually brought the end of directories and yellow pages. An Uber would do the same to private taxi businesses.

The GQ companies often don't even make money; that is, they take years to come up with a value capture methodology, but they do put an end to businesses with years of legacies. To explain further, the GQ companies do not necessarily come out with a better product or greater expertise. They meet a customer's need that was left unaddressed by the expertise. Amazon, Google, Uber, Netflix and iTunes were all, for example, built around ease and simplicity. People like me still cherish the experience of going to a bookstore and surfing endlessly, but we do not do it anymore. That is the GQ. The GQ puts a firm in a position to define the future trends and capture the white spaces.

It is useful to think of value creation in terms of GQ. What little value creation that need not even be the best product or service meets a customer need overlooked by the giants? The GQ or future strategies from thereon are not about cost, price or service models. They are all about mass customer acquisition. The business models, at least initially, are not built around value capture, though they should be. They are built around capital capture. And in capturing capital again, value creation trumps value capture. How else does anyone explain WhatsApp operating with a small team in a small office with virtually zero revenue being acquired for billions of dollars? That is the GQ. The post office has all the expertise and excellence to deliver a message. It is profitable in most countries. It creates immense value. Yet it is an isolated expertise, and so the capital will flow towards the brilliance.

SELL
THE PROBLEM
YOU SOLVE
NOT
THE PRODUCT

PROBLEM PERCEPTION IS
THE DIFFERENTIATOR

Try answering these questions. Ninety-nine per cent of businesses cannot go beyond number 3.

1. What does your business do?
2. Why is it that you can do what you do?
3. What unique problem does it solve that no one else currently does?
4. Why does the problem matter?
5. Who says that the problem matters?
6. Who does the problem matter to the most?
7. Is the size enough for it to be a large problem to solve?
8. Why is the solution reliable?
9. Why will the solution be preferred?
10. How will it be monetized?
11. What should be the ROI (for adoption)?
12. What is the ROI?

In recent times, we have witnessed the problem of the COVID-19 pandemic. The problem perception is so huge that even 65 per cent of solution reliability has governments spending billions. The odds are that if someone came up to you with a solution that said there is a 65 per cent chance that they may solve your problem, you are likely to never see them again. Then again, it depends on the problem at hand.

Companies today have an excessive focus on digitalization and technology. This is often equated to innovation and transformation. This is herd-based thinking. Innovation was always and will always be led by human beings. Technology is a tool. The reason it is led by human beings is because human beings have the power to perceive.

Problem perception is a not a matter of ideation and brain storming in a room full of executives. It is about the connection with reality. Most decision-makers, founders, business people and leaders rarely connect with reality beyond a computer-generated report. Their problem perception then is guided by and limited to data. They are always going to be up against the one with the GQ.

You will only ever perceive a unique problem if you observe people interacting with the existing solutions. Steve Jobs's original perception of iPhone was out of an observation that people are spending most of their time on a handheld device that needs two hands to operate. Apple created the initial iPhone which could be operated by a single hand.

People buy solutions, products or services in response to a problem. The problem needs to remain relevant for the solution to have meaning. This implies that problem search must be a constant capability available to a business to sustain and innovate.

While writing this book, for example, I observed people on how they interact with books. People hardly ever read a book end to end. They begin and then they leave it midway. Either they get what they want out of it and lose interest or they have to wait too long to get what they want out of it and lose interest.

With that problem perception, I decided to write a book which has a takeaway in each section that covers not more than two pages.

DON'T DEDUCE GROWTH
MULTIPLY IT

MULTIPLICITY OF VALUE CREATION LEADS TO MASS ADOPTION

Problems are everywhere. No one is completely happy with anything they have in their life. At a business front, no customer is totally happy with any product or service that they use. There must be a gap to fill.

Value creation needs to be treated as a multiplicative exercise than an incremental one. In business, we are conditioned to look at goals as a deduction of previous efforts, and, therefore, our activities become incremental; we only solve a small problem or better a solution to an existing problem.

The GQ companies went about it differently. They attacked multiple levels of problems. Typically, there are five kinds of problems.

1. The core functional problem: This is a problem related to the use of existing product or solution. What is the missing existing solution that can make it easier or better for a consumer if it were to be fixed? For example, Reliance Jio's strategy in India was to make telecommunication cheaper and spread it to attract the non-paying rural customer.

2. Related problems: These are problems related to the core problem. Amazon started as an online bookstore but now has to solve the problem of shipping and supply chain. It is the shipping and supply chain capability that actually enables Amazon to become the giant business it is.

3. Emotional problems: Adopting innovations and products is actually the first emotional decision for a consumer than a physical one. What are, then, the positive and negative emotional relationships people have with existing solutions? How will you build an emotional appeal to better or overcome the current connections people have? Companies

like Coca Cola have invested decades in building an emotional relationship with the masses. The newer entrants are faced with a daunting task of competing emotionally. However, cafeterias like Starbucks had found an emotional space to acquire the beverage market share.

4. Consumption chain problems: Consumption chain or expansion of value creation to multiple networks is one of the key strategies adopted by future trend companies. Apple expanded their potential to developers through the app store, Amazon through sellers, Netflix through participation with content creators and so on.

5. Financial problems: These are problems related to purchasing. A consumer may want it, but can they afford it? Financial structuring of a solution is as important as consumption-related challenges if they are to be mass adopted. Everyone wants to own a house, for example, but financial structuring doesn't allow it—a situation that is absolutely ripe for disruption.

A brilliant model is one that can transcend traditional models and create value across a spectrum of perceived problems, rather than just create expertise around a single area. Value creation is a holistic activity, and it needn't end at all. When one examines the multiplicity of problems that a human being is surrounded by, the value creation is almost a timeless activity and one that is really the only competitive advantage.

"On paper we have the perfect team."

AND THEN THERE IS MARKETING; SUCCESS IS NOT AUTOMATIC

People become open to innovation when the problems are marketed well. Take, for example, the worldwide focus on United Nations' sustainability goals. Almost every established company seems to be in a race to establish credibility. Even nations are in a race to become carbon neutral. There aren't too many credible solutions available, by the way, to achieve these yet. However, the problem has been marketed so remarkably well that any solution would be saleable.

Consider the Apple watch, the largest selling wearable gadget. When people started getting addicted to iPhone screens and data of how smartphone screens deteriorate consumer's heath became news, Apple found the opportunity even in this predicament. It came out with smartwatches using health as the primary leverage to sell its watches. Microsoft and Adobe projected owning expensive software as a problem. This problem was well travelled globally through people whose work required using these software. Then came the hugely successful subscription model that lets you use the software for a monthly fee. Over 30 per cent of the new revenues in either of these companies come from the cloud services.

Success is not automatic because value has been created. Many creators have been heartbroken, not because they couldn't create but because they assumed people would flock over.

For all of Apple's creations, Steve Jobs never missed the stage to showcase.

Innovation and creativity are low-probability games because of the uniqueness and unpredictability they offer. Marketing is the balance of probability. If the problem is marketed well to the extent of being adopted as a universal truth, then the solution need not even deliver for it to be adopted. This is evident in politics all over the world.

Before a consumer tastes the value, they have to be troubled by the problem. Are you aware of the real problem you are solving and are you able to market the problem? As long as the problem is relevant, you are too.

Problem perception is a unique skill needed to create innovations. That is precisely the reason problems need marketing. If it is a unique skill, then it certainly will not be a majority trait. How will the people know that there is a problem? Steve Jobs once commented that customers don't know what they want. Deducing from that, it is quite evident that customers usually don't perceive problems well. Although once they do, existing loyalties almost seem to disappear.

Business communities generally perceive marketing to be a tool to brand or popularize products by highlighting solutions and uniqueness. That works. The winners who take it all though highlight problems.

FedEx became the market leader on a promise of next-day delivery. That in itself was a problem statement. It made people aware that there is a problem. The selection capability on Amazon itself revealed a problem that people were not aware of. The ease of a simple search box on Google made people aware of the problem of searching for something or someone. Skype's functionality of calls over wireless made people aware of the expense of making international calls. Most recently, the adoption of technology for virtual meetings may have made over 50 per cent of business travel redundant even after things become normal.

People buy problems first, then the solutions. Doesn't it then make sense to market the problem first? Traditional marketing strategies may build brands but not businesses. Businesses get built by solving problems. The problems must be validated and adopted by the masses for the business to have a chance of reaching that mass.

The assumption that I am good and so eventually others will see the goodness is a fool's paradise. Even Gandhi had to form alliances with newspapers to free a country that wanted to be freed. It is not automated. Value creation is half the job done, which may not be adopted if the problem has not been marketed.

DESIRE
IS INSIDE - OUT

PERCEIVE A PROBLEM; DON'T INVENT IT

Most people and organizations' goals are born out of their desires and ambitions. Desire is always accompanied with fear (of not getting the results). Desire invents the world inside out.

For example, one may have a desire to be the number one company in an industry. Thereafter, the world is inside out. It may provoke questions such as: What do we do to become number one? How do we acquire market shares? And what kinds of investments are needed?

Desire invents problems that are central to you and transports them out to the real world for exploitation. This intent mostly does not allow for a true perception of what actually is because the perception is coloured by what one wants out of reality.

Politics is a great example of it. In every country, political parties are motivated to fight elections to gain power. They see several issues that trouble people. These issues are used to form a narrative to win but rarely become a problem for politicians to solve, unless it becomes a threat to them losing their power.

A majority of the world is driven by desire and, therefore, the majority doesn't perceive unique problems. They perceive selfish ones. These are common—more money, more security, more success, more power, more titles, more houses, more cars, etc.

Perceiving means to become aware of what actually is, not what is ought to be. It is when the desire lens shifts to that of concern that our mind allows us to perceive reality for what it is. Within the lens of desire, the primary concern is self, and so the problems perceived are inside out. Within the lens of concern, the primary focus is the pain of others and that allows for a perception of reality.

How do your strengths or expertise interact with the concerns of people or customers around you? Are you using it to invent solutions to fulfil desires, or are you using it to solve a problem?

Let's see an example. According to the UN Food and Agricultural Organization, saving the world's food waste would help feed two billion people. That's more than twice the number of under-nourished people across the globe. This basically means that wasted food around the world is enough for no one to remain hungry, ever. Hunger kills more people in the world than any disease or problem. Yet many people sleep with an empty stomach and many of us sleep with bins full of food that was enough to feed the hungry.

Technology and science today have the means to develop a solution to solve this. We have the supply chain intelligence to take the waste to the needy. Yet we don't. Why?

The reason is simple, from politicians to businesses, from governments to individuals, we are governed by desire and not concern. Concern perceives problems. Solving problems need not be charity or social responsibility projects. Two billion is a massive customer base.

BUT
WHY DO YOU WANT 'THAT' ROPE

CREATE AND CAPTURE ARE SEPARATE WORLDS

People playing tug of war are insanely occupied and busy in trying to get a piece of the rope, because they don't know how to create another one.

Value creation is separate from value capture. Creation is in a sense expanding the size of the pie. Capture is getting a share of the pie. Balance sheets reflect what is captured. People obsessed with capturing are not creators. They usually don't know how to expand the pie. Yet the last two decades have shown us that it is the businesses who have expanded the pie, created markets that were non-existent or created solutions that weren't even present in the last century have created the most valued institutions.

When value capture interferes with value creation, and when the intent is higher on capture than creation, innovation will become a backbencher.

To create value first means to solve unsolved problems, expand the pie, shift the lenses of perception and then create solutions that are novel and useful. Once expanded, the game may shift to claiming value, and that is a separate skill. In a business, both have to run parallelly. Unfortunately, many businesses become about simply 'capturing' value. While they sustain and make money, they add no value to the world because it doesn't matter beyond certain semantics, whether they exist or not. No one cried over the Andersons and Enrons of the world when they shut down. It is the Kodaks and Nokias that still intrigue and trouble people.

Claiming value is important because it provides the resources to be able to go on creating value. This simple distinction is absent in most business paradigms. Claiming value is not just for reporting healthy balance sheets and inflated profits—that is the purely dominant 'desire' world. Claiming value is a source for creating further value. It is this chain of create–capture–create that creates brilliance. The chain of create–capture–capture creates stress and pressure. It may lead to a bank balance but the whole system in which this operates, that is, the organization, employees, customers, vendors and their families, get educated to simply capture value. In the end, the system will get consumed by the very selfishness it created. It always remains vulnerable to the GQ because it doesn't have any.

CAPTURE
CAPTURES
CREATIVITY

BEHIND THE CAPTURE BARS

In Stage 1, it was discussed that the big picture is in the 'and' and not in the 'or', that is, the brilliance lies in integrating and not in isolating.

The question, therefore, is not whether to have a strategy to create or capture value. The challenge lies in doing both. This is nuanced though.

Most of the times in organizations, once the capture value stage sets in, creativity and innovation become the prisoners. Innovation then occurs within the lens of capturing value. This is similar to, let's say, a prisoner who is captured. The prisoner can still be innovative but remains behind the bars. Similarly, once the intent of the organization shifts to capturing value, it may still be innovative but only within the context of capturing value. For example, a company manufacturing watches may be very innovative in its designs and technology or anything that it feels will sustain their market shares and margins but will rarely be the company to innovate (e.g., the smartwatch) their way into the white spaces.

Success comes with the shareholder's curse. Eventually, a firm or even an individual must capture value to be considered successful. Oftentimes, capturing value takes the focus away from creating further value and one then becomes a part of the Red Queen's race.

Figure 5.2 sums this up. Creation, as discussed earlier, is a result of unique problem perception. At the initial stages, the solutions may be theoretical, but as the creator's journey progresses, these take the form of solutions that may be introduced into the market. Capture, on the other side, is born out of ambitions. Capturing may mean trading off on the values of creation itself. Usually, these are conflicting realities. An organization may value creation more or capture more, and both sides will usually

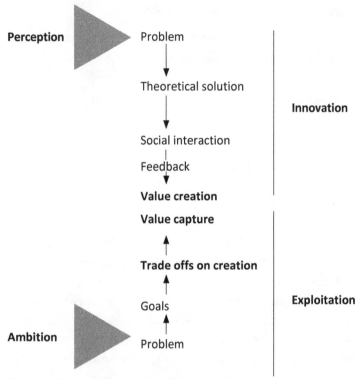

Figure 5.2 Perception vs Ambition

represent a conflict. As Mr O's story tells us, these conflicts need not be regressive; they can be an opportunity where everyone wins too.

Pharmaceutical companies are an example, where creation happens within the capture umbrella. Petroleum companies (or OPEC nations) are examples where the strategies are heavily centred on capture intents. WhatsApp and some new-age technology businesses were examples of creators who didn't have the 'capture' strategy and yet were acquired by the ones who could foresee capturing value through those acquisitions. Companies like Google and Apple have almost perfected ambidextrous structures where creation and capture coexist.

Value sustainability is a function of create + capture. Leadership, going forward into this century, will increasingly be about skills that can manage the conflicting realities of a dual structure within the same organization. The pace of innovation means that a company may no longer have the luxury to not innovate. The same pace dictates that innovations must translate into revenue to provide resources for the ones to keep innovating. In a nutshell, brilliance is not optional but essential.

BRILLIANCE CREDO

1. What is your mechanism to observe problems that are out there in action within your domain and your industry?

2. How will you empirically validate the problem observed?

3. What is your strategy for continuous knowledge acquisition?

4. What is your strategy to build a capability for innovation using the acquired knowledge?

5. What GQ can be applied to the problem perceived? In other words, what is a small innovation that can have a massive impact?

6. How do you create multiplicity of values across the problem chain?

7. What is your strategy to market problems so that they are mass adopted?

STAGE SIX

DECISION-MAKING

Choosing and Connecting

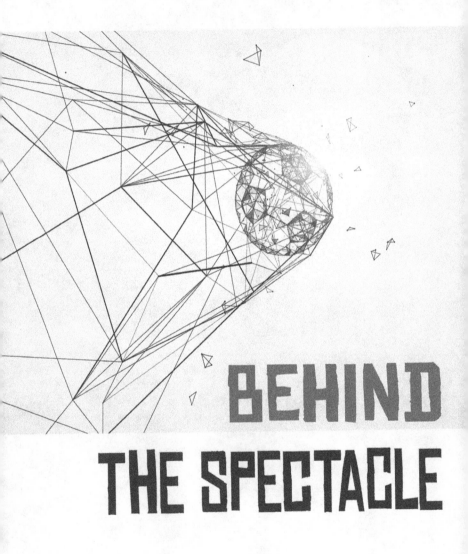

BEHIND
THE SPECTACLE

EVERYTHING IS A DECISION

No effect occurs by itself. It is a deflection mechanism at play to attribute outcomes to luck or chance. Every outcome in life or in business is rooted in a decision. It may become difficult to trace the effect to a decision because of the complexities involved in doing so. Even then it doesn't mean that it is not so.

There is an old story of the world heavyweight champion—a man named Floyd Patterson. One time in the ring, a few seconds later, Floyd crashed and was no longer the heavyweight champion. Ingemar Johannsson was crowned. No heavyweight champion in history had ever won back the crown. Floyd was written off by every expert. But Floyd made a public statement: 'I will do it.'

He took the help of former champion Joe Louis who said, 'To win you have to change your mental attitude. The way to get Ingemar is to get him to miss. Then step inside. Control your urge to hit. Practice.' Floyd Patterson made him miss. He didn't take a proper shot until the fifth round. Floyd won.

Patterson made to the press before the bout, when they were clicking pictures. He said, 'The most important thing you can't get any picture of; because the most important thing for me is my mental attitude.'

The world sees the spectacle of results. What lies behind the spectacle are choices, just like Patterson chose to reclaim his crown. He chose to put in the training. He chose the advice he may or may not follow. He chose the strategy in the ring. He chose to be patient for five rounds. Of course, he could have lost too. Choices or decisions shape outcomes. Yes, situations appear before us that may be undesirable. How we deal with those situations or not is still a choice.

If you are unhealthy, obese and overweight, you chose to live in a certain way to get to that reality.

If you are broke, you chose to make certain use of money to get there.

If you are jobless, you are choosing to wait in your home.

If you are in troubled relationships, you are choosing to stay in them.

If you are unhappy, you are choosing to put up with certain environments that produce that result for you.

You get the point? Good luck or bad luck, recession or growth, as the days pass into weeks, or as the weeks pass into months or years, the choice is always yours. You are the creator of your environment.

Why do some people like Floyd create an environment, while others fall and accept what they get?

Why do some organizations thrive on competition, while others are crushed?

Why does one entrepreneur beat unfathomable odds, while others give up?

Why do some parents rear children who are good citizens in neighbourhoods riddled with violence and drugs?

Why does an individual beat the odds, overcoming an abusive childhood when most do not?

Only one in seven people attempting to climb Mt Everest actually succeeds. What is so special about them?

Why do so many gifted or high IQ people fall far short of their potential?

I invite you to read through a quote from John Greenleaf Whittier, *Maud Muller*, 1856, Stanza 53

> For of all sad words of tongue or pen,
> the saddest are these, **'It might have been!'**

Some people choose not to quit! They adapt. They move. They call time on actions. They have had enough. In the end, failure is a decision to give up, just as success may be an outcome of persevering.

ENERGY > EFFECT

POTENTIAL DOESN'T MEAN WHAT YOU THINK IT MEANS

Schools aim to do it. Jobs promise to do it. Lifestyle gurus and self-help handbooks proclaim that they'll do it. They'll all help you to reach your potential, or realize your potential, or release or achieve or free your potential. But what is your potential, and what does it mean to achieve it? If your answer to this question is something vague along the lines of 'It's what I can do, and it means I can, um, do it,' you're not alone. Many people have the idea that their potential is something positive, or remember school teachers telling them that they were wasting it, but would struggle to define it clearly. So while schools and jobs (and self-help books) can indeed help you reach your potential, you might not benefit from their help unless you know what that really means. We say that effects are result of decisions. However, what is the relationship between potential and the ability to create that effect?

If you studied science at school, you might remember the concept of potential energy. A weight when held in air has potential energy. Why? Well, if you release the weight, it falls to the ground, makes a loud noise and possibly causes some damage to your flooring. It clearly has got some energy when it's falling, and that energy can't have appeared from nowhere, so when it's suspended, the energy must still be in it, even if you can't see any evidence of it. That's potential energy. Why is this reminder of physics lessons relevant? People talk about their potential as if it's something they can do. But when that weight has potential energy, it's not doing anything. That's the important information that most people don't understand.

Potential is the set of circumstances and the attitude that enables you to do something. Achieving your potential is your first step, not your destination. Potential is when the available energy has the ability to cause an effect. Once the effect is caused and the energy is dissipated, the potential is exhausted.

People and organizations build up potential and then strategize to exploit it. They forget to keep in mind that potential is ahead of the results.

Potential here is referred to as energy to create an effect. What is energy made up of? In very simplistic terms, the energy is made up of beliefs, knowledge, attitude, ability and habits or routines. For most people, all of these are static realities. People form a set of beliefs on what their future holds for them or what they can or not do. Knowledge is equated for most to formal education and work experiences thereon. Attitudes are mostly shaped by events and outcomes that people get as a result of putting this knowledge to work. Abilities or newer unrelated skills are rarely acquired. The sum of these leads to routines and habits in lives which are quite predictable leading into the future. The energy to create effects does not really proportionately increase with time. People do create effects for themselves. Of course, you are better off than to say when you were 5 or 10 years ago. But what is your energy reservoir looking like?

The incremental nature of life, results and business can be understood by understanding potential like this. In the absence of a mass of energy available to create a massive impact, the existing potential creates an incremental one.

This doesn't mean hoarding abilities. Rather, it implies enhancing them. For example, availability of capital has potential. If that capital is put to use, it no longer has potential; it will now produce an effect. This doesn't mean that we don't put the capital to use; rather, it implies that we do it in a manner that capital may always remain available too, either by judicious employment or by earning more.

Erosion or exhaustion of potential is also a result of decision-making.

Do you have a surplus of knowledge available in different streams and directions? How much time do you invest in learning, self-educating, developing expert levels of insights into a subject versus activities such as mindless meetings, televisions and entertainment? That is a decision.

Do you constantly question your beliefs about things that matter? Beliefs, at the end of the day, are just assumptions. They may or may not be true. Do you challenge them or accept them? The world believed in the 1950s that a human body cannot run a mile in under four minutes. Universal truth! Yet Roger Bannister challenged it. What do you believe about the past, present and the future, and why? Whatever you believe is a decision.

How do you deal with events and outcomes? Do you accept it as an end result or like Patterson challenge it to turn it around? That is attitude, and attitude itself is shaped by what you have in the energy store. Again, that is a decision.

What new skills did you acquire this year? Or the last year? Or the year before that? Can you think of some? Which new skills will you acquire in the coming year? The year after that? Can you think of some? Those right there were and are decisions for upgrading or exhausting potential.

Do your routines permit you to add knowledge, beliefs and skills to your reservoir, or do your routines deplete them? Routines are decisions you take on autopilot every single day.

Strategically, an organization's ability to create an effect must always remain far ahead of the created effects. Look around you. Study the people you admire. Ask a simple question. Did this person have potential; that is, do their abilities to create even further effects outweigh the existing effects? You will probably get the answer to why you look up to them.

Take for example, Steve Jobs. If he didn't meet the end that he did, wouldn't we have seen more revolutionary products than we have from Apple?

Would Gandhi have stopped at just giving India freedom?

Would Schumacher have simply retired and become oblivious?

Would Walt Disney have created the next thing after Disney Land or stopped right there?

Just like that weight being held in mid-air, you are full of potential when you build up energy by creating something new in you and in your company. Potential is not an end result because it is forever active but it surely is a decision you take or not. Everyone can achieve their potential and everyone does. It is the next step that decides the next levels of outcomes.

ARCHETYPE

THE HERO'S JOURNEY

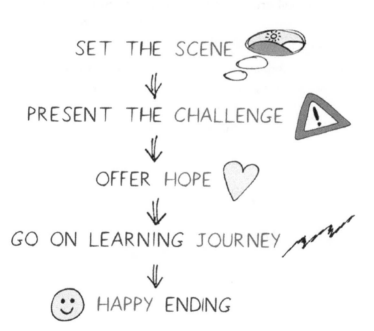

SET THE SCENE

⇓

PRESENT THE CHALLENGE

⇓

OFFER HOPE

⇓

GO ON LEARNING JOURNEY

⇓

HAPPY ENDING

LIMITATIONS OF CONTEXT

Decision-making in an organization is generally understood as key decisions made by top management members. There are three dimensions to real-life strategic situations. These are strategy context, strategy content and strategy process. Based on these arguments, a study was conducted on the analysis of peer-reviewed papers in top-tier academic and practitioner journals. The study recommended a framework organized into context, content, process and outcome (Figure 6.1; Papadakis et al., 2010).

Context: The context can be broadly understood in terms of the environment (competitive environment), organization (internal structures), nature of the decision (impact) and top management characteristics (CEO and top management team personalities and backgrounds).

Content: Content is the content of the decision or the specific decisions taken, for example, the strategies to create new

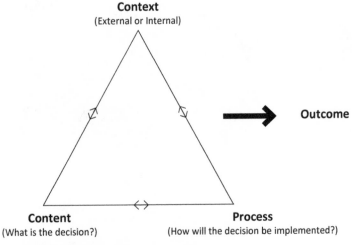

Figure 6.1 Decision-making Process

Source: Walia (2021).

products, diversify or differentiate or achieve cost leadership at the business level.

Process: Process is concerned with how the decision will translate into action through the selection of ideas, management of politics, evolution of consensus, communication, allocation of resources, monitoring, control and evaluation.

Outcome: Outcome refers to the outcome of the decision in terms of the decision's effectiveness (speed and quality) or is measured in terms of financial performance (growth in profits or sales) or even in terms of public image and goodwill generated.

The leaders of any organization shape the direction of the firm based on how they prioritize the interests of different stakeholders such as shareholders, employees, customers and society. However, in a study exploring the influence of the CEO and the leadership teams on the process of decision-making, it was noted that (a) CEOs had more influence on the process and (b) the context in which the decisions are set has a greater influence than even the CEO or other stakeholders (Papadakis, 2002).

External environments such as the economy, market conditions and competitive landscape are the most popular contexts under which the decisions take place. These contexts determine the psychological pressures on the decision-makers to prioritize direction. These then guide the direction of internal firm realities, such as the culture, resistance to change, complexities, appetite for risk, intelligence, decision-making styles, need for control or power, politics within a firm, or even education backgrounds and personal values of the decision-makers.

In the end, the external context or the pressures of the external context ensures that almost everything else is negotiable.

While context is important and organizations must address the external demands—else, it may not even survive—context has a blind side. The context itself limits what decision-makers can or cannot see. This is well explained by the Monkey Business Illusion (available on YouTube[1]) and based on the book, *The Invisible Gorilla*.

In the illustration, the viewers are presented with the context of basketball players, half of them dressed in whites and the other half dressed in black, dribbling the ball and passing it among themselves. The viewers are asked to count the number of times the ball is passed among them. So taken in by the context of what to focus on and what not to, over 80 per cent of the viewers fail to notice a prominent gorilla dancing on the screen, right in front of them.

The limitation of the context is that we may miss the obvious.

IBM didn't think that there was a world market for computers.

Harvard Economic Society thought that the 1929 Depression was beyond the realms of possibility.

Apple fired Steve Jobs.

India and Pakistan continue to fight wars over the territory that was shared for almost 2,000 years.

In the recent past, we have seen that the giants of Wall Street take hours to become history, not because they didn't know how to capitalize on external context but because that's all that they could see.

---

[1] www.youtube.com/watch?v=IGQmdoK_ZfY

HEADLINES

IS NOT
THE REAL
STORY

CONTEXTUALIZE POTENTIAL

Every company has similar people, backgrounds, opportunities, environments, facilities, markets, economies, technologies and alike. Yet there are some who achieve a thousand or even a million times more than others. Those achievements make headlines. Headlines are not the real story. The singular context of achievement is not the most ideal one. Let's take a look at the potential-context matrix.

The 'and' factor of brilliance is very evident in the potential–context matrix in Figure 6.2. When the decision-makers adopt an external economic context to a lower degree, and the potential (as defined in this book) is also at a lower degree, the decision-makers tend to be reactive exploiters. Reactive exploiters are chasers in a Red Queen's race. They will be compelled to react to the innovations of the marketplace and their competition in order to survive. Once Apple came up with the smartphone, the other manufacturers were left in this quadrant.

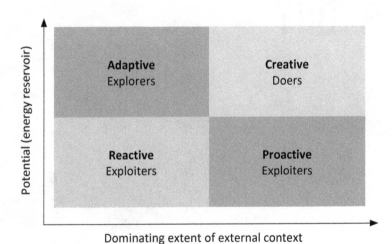

Figure 6.2 Potential and Context

When the degree of focus on external context is high and the potential is lower, the decision-makers tend to be proactive exploiters. They lead the exploitation in the marketplace, and their strategies and decisions are aimed to exploit and sustain, for example, tobacco companies.

When the potential availability is high and the contextual focus is lower, the decision-makers tend to be adaptive explorers. These companies will respond to the exploiters by adapting newer products or solutions. For example, Alibaba started manufacturing or assembling ventilators in response to COVID-19 pandemic.

It is when the high potential combines with high degree of contextual focus that decision-makers tend to be creative doers. That is, they lead markets with innovative solutions that capture market shares and leave other firms in any of the other three quadrants behind.

Companies can transcend between any of these quadrants at different stages of their evolution. It is absolutely possible for a company to be a creative doer and get reduced to being a reactive exploiter, for example, Nokia and Blackberry. However, building up potential helps the turnaround. Fujifilm and Phillips, in similar situations, built the potential to serve the health industry. Fujifilm was in a similar position to Kodak but discovered unmet needs related to their products within the medical industry. Philips separated its core lighting business from the healthcare division, transforming itself into primarily a healthcare technology company.

Very few companies focus on building real muscle for the future. Most companies get consumed by the context itself. It is not that they are not successful. Reactive and proactive exploiters may be very successful companies and businesses. We are, however, dealing in this book with brilliance. Brilliance lies in having a sound business model to profit from the present but also, simultaneously, shaping the future for the entire industry, altogether.

A critical factor in building a company to do that is decision-making. Things that you say 'yes' and 'no' to determine the quadrants you belong to. One of the assumptions that the lower quadrants make is that potential is static and can always be built up or acquired. In this process, the decision-makers end up with a culture that will never be able to value the creative ones. Contrary to that, one of the assumptions of the upper quadrants could be that success of a product or solution is automatic because the product itself is so damn good. This is the creator's heartbreak moment because that too doesn't happen. Therefore, decision-making is as much about consciously challenging assumptions as it is about directionally shaping strategy.

ALIGNMENT
IS MEDIOCRITY'S SYNONYM

THE VICTIM OF DECISION-MAKING

In negotiations, there is a concept called subjective value. Subjective value is built up by developing trust and goodwill with the other side. In decision-making, this may well be understood as notional subjective value, that is, a false pretence of trust and goodwill to avoid a conflict.

Within an organization, decision-making tends to be, at least, notionally collective. A leadership team or think tank represents different thought worlds such as sales, planning, technical and manufacturing. These different thought worlds are likely to lead to differences in creative suggestions made by each person, which generally means an occurrence of conflicting frames. In the interest of larger organizational goals, a negotiated order is likely to emerge. The individual or collective perception of external context has a significant influence on such negotiations. Often, a decision that emerges is dependent on the frame or individual which had more power. Context is used here as a way of aligning everyone to a common picture.

This negotiated order or decision is mostly a result of agreeing on common denominators. Decision-makers may give up conflicting positions to create a false sense of subjective value, that is, to align with the boss (or authority), to appear group-friendly, to build trust, to secure one's position, to maintain a degree of acceptable status or to not appear misaligned to the majority. This notional subjective value has real value too. It helps in executing the decision. However, the notional subjective value has a victim too. The victim is possibility.

Behaviourally, when there is a blind side, it would need another to take a conflicting position to show the blind side to a person. This is where subjective value really comes in handy—that there is enough trust to confront a problem. Notional subjective value falls short in its ability to achieve that and, therefore, decision-makers compromise.

Conflicts, contrary to normative belief systems, are absolutely essential in generating possibilities. In an empirical study, it was noted that negotiated orders or alignment may help in execution, but it has an adverse effect on innovation (West, 2002).

There is a huge difference between doing the right thing and doing the acceptable thing. Group decision-making processes in organizations mostly align to the acceptable thing. They remain predictable. They remain mediocre and incremental, much like cutting Mr O's orange into half.

Examine a conflict from the point of view of subjective value (relationships) and objective value (goals) as shown in Figure 6.3. One could assert their way on goal achievement, adopt the other

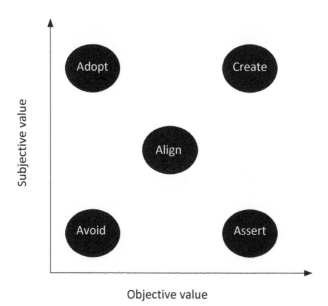

Figure 6.3 Cross Section of Value in Decision-making

side's solutions and avoid the conflict altogether, or as most decision-making processes do, align to a negotiated order. Compromise is not a solution, it is a compromise. Real value creation happens with integration.

Exploration and exploitation are themselves conflicts. The idea cannot be to align with creating either an exploitative strategy or an explorative one. The required leadership strategy is to create a big picture by combining both. This is where one needs potential, in the form of an energy reservoir to have the knowledge, skills and abilities, to convert conflict into a problem and find solutions, rather than agreements.

THE DECISION-MAKING CREDO

1. Have you built in time to focus on the building up of potential? Have you lightened your load?

   a. Is action required?

   b. Is there a need to make a decision?

   c. Who should make the decision?

   d. Does this need a group?

   e. Is there a cost to pay for alignment?

2. Do your culture and organization support making the right decisions and not just the acceptable ones?

   a. What's the real issue? What are you trying to accomplish?

   b. How does the solution enter the quadrant of 'creative doers'? What are the minimum results required and what organizational commitment is needed to achieve them? What are the risks?

   c. Have you fully considered the entire range of alternatives in order to choose the best one? Do you have a contingency plan?

   d. What opportunities do the biggest conflicts present?

3. Is the organization willing to commit to the decision once it has been made?

   a. Are you willing to opt for the bold move to get the required results?

   b. Can you marshal support for your decision within the organization and not rehash the decision?

   c. Can you integrate the visionary and the practical?

4. As decisions are made, are resources allocated to 'degenerate into work?'

    a. Have you gained the commitment and the capacity of the resources which will convert the decision into action?

    b. Have you put mechanisms in place to provide organized tracking and feedback such that it doesn't just generate notional subjective value?

REFERENCES

Papadakis, V. M., & Barwise, P. (2002). How much do CEOs and top managers matter in strategic decision making? *British Journal of Management, 13*(1), 83–95.

Papadakis, V., Thanos, I., & Barwise, P. (2010). Research on strategic decision: Taking stock and looking ahead. In P. C. Nutt & D. C. Wilson (Eds.), *Handbook of decision* making (pp. 31–70). John Wiley & Sons.

Walia, C. (2021). Creativity and strategic decision making by top management teams. In *Creativity and strategy*. Springer Nature.

West, M. A. (2002). Sparkling fountains or stagnant ponds: An integrative model of creativity and innovation implementation in work groups. *International Association for Applied Psychology, 51*(3), 355–424.

THE CULTURAL JIGSAW

BEWARE OF ASSUMPTIONS !

WHATEVER

•••••◆•••••

YOU ASSUME TO BE POSSIBLE

OR IMPOSSIBLE

WILL HAVE A TENDENCY

TO BECOME REAL FOR YOU

WHAT IS CULTURE?

Things that get done are execution. What about the things that do not get done but people made efforts towards completing? Isn't that execution too? In sports matches, one hears the losing side's captain or coach lament often, 'We couldn't execute our plans.' Imagine a football match. That is 90 minutes of execution, regardless of the outcome. Everyone in your organization goes to work, 8–10 hours a day. Whether they do something productive or not, that is execution. No one really goes to work to deliberately fail. Yet they do fail. People execute and express themselves within a set of boundaries. On the playing field, people execute; behind the playing field, people decide the boundaries within which they must execute. Boundaries override the potential in most people's lives and in most organizations. The boundaries are the culture within which we live.

Very literally, the change of boundaries for people could mean a complete change of results. The same people who weren't able to accomplish anything in one company may go on to flourish in another. The same people who struggled in one country go on to become leaders in another. The same people who failed in a certain environment dominate another in a different time.

Etymologically, culture is derived from the word 'cultivate'. Cultivate means 'the act of preparing the earth for the crop'. This is the simplest way to understand culture. Culture is the act of preparing the individual, teams and organization for execution and results.

Every organization has a culture, much like every family has one. It may not be known, it may not be documented, but everyone within the family inherently knows the boundaries of being there. These need not even be explicitly communicated or agreed to and yet they move over from one generation to another. The rebels will rebel, fight and go live on their own; the family lives and the culture dies. The rebels choose a different one but make no mistake; they too live within a boundary system, just another one. Very often, a family has a different set of rules for siblings living under the same roof. These boundaries often dictate the realization of potential for each of those.

What is the need for these boundaries? In a very simplistic sense, boundaries give control, direction and continuance of tradition. Organizations need to govern and, hence, need control mechanisms. They need to give people and teams of people a sense of direction and goals and, therefore, need to somewhat define what can be done or not. Leaders in an organization come with beliefs about what will lead to success and so they desire for setting certain routines in place. Routines are traditions. The question is not that whether you will have a culture or not. The question is what culture you will have and how you will create it deliberately. Before we delve into that, let's first define the culture itself.

An organization works within an external environment. This was discussed as context earlier. The external environment is the markets, economy, regulations, competitive landscape and alike. This is an ever-evolving dynamic world and has its own set of complexities. The individual in an organization is the internal context who has to solve problems arising from the external environment and formulate plans and strategies. The individual doesn't work alone. The individual is a part of groups or teams, often multiple teams. Each of these teams has an impact on the working of the other teams. The teams may also be external to the organization in the form of partners. The collection of these teams forms the organization. The organization represents a structure, strategy and reward mechanisms that are applicable to individuals therein.

At every step of this dynamic (as shown in Figure 7.1), that is, flow of information, formulation of plans and execution, from external

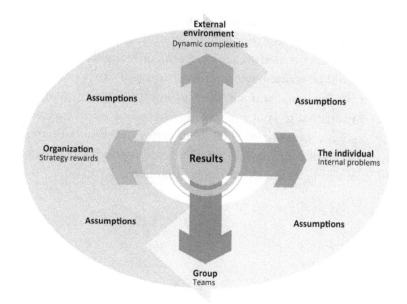

Figure 7.1 Elements of Culture

environment to individuals to teams to organization, people make assumptions. For example, the external environment is largely the same to everyone in an industry but they draw different conclusions, goals and strategies. Why? Because they make different assumptions. The individuals adopt different styles and approach different problems to solve or solve problems differently because of the assumptions they draw. The teams make assumptions of what is important, doable and acceptable and act accordingly. The organization's leadership makes assumptions about the future, stakeholders and their importance and deliberates accordingly. These assumptions are unwritten rules. The set of these assumptions define the boundary conditions. These assumptions, based on which the players act (or not), are the organization's culture.

Culture is the unwritten rules of success within an organization's ecosystem. The unwritten rules are the boundaries under which people act. The unwritten rules, and not the written ones, determine the culture. The written laws, for example, are the same for everyone in a country. The interpretation and usage are not. People act on interpretations, on the meaning they make of what is said or written, rather than what is said or written. As a reader of this book, you are likely to interpret what is written here and adapt it to your reality. Your adaptations are you adjusting to your boundaries. The boundaries are the collective assumptions of your organization. These assumptions will dictate the execution and not the words written here.

TRUST

TEAMWORK

RESPONSIBILITY

CUSTOMERS

ETHICS

INNOVATION

COACHING

GOALS

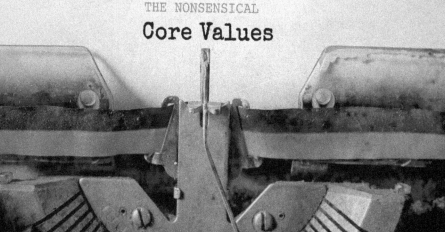

THE NONSENSICAL
Core Values

ICU: INAUTHENTIC CULTURE UNIT

Enron had nice-sounding core values. They were integrity, communication, respect and excellence. Arthur Andersen had them. They were about 'think straight, talk straight'; duty, integrity, ethics, trust; and one firm, one voice.

One hundred and fifty-eight years of the Lehman Brothers were backed by a solid written code of conduct that all the employees supposedly followed. One of the statements in that code read, 'The lynchpins of that trust are our ethical standards and behavior. We must always do business in a manner that protects and promotes the interest of our clients' (Stevens & Buechler, 2013)

Popularized in the last two–four decades, an organization's core values have almost become synonymous with our understanding of its culture. This is one of the central actions that all human resources leaders tend to drive alongside the purpose of an organization that projects it as some divine interventionist on behalf of the creator. The walls of most organizations on this planet are plastered with words 'honesty' and 'integrity'. Behind those walls sit the legal departments who are constantly working to find loopholes in the laws to abandon contracts and save taxes. These walls house cabins in which executives strategize to sell products that are fundamentally harmful to human beings or are made in a manner that is. Do core values have any sanctity? Are they a fair representation of an organization's culture?

They would be if they were non-negotiable, but are they? Are your values non-negotiable? If you ask anyone what your values are, chances are that everyone will narrate values such as honesty, trust and respect. Is any of this non-negotiable or is everything situational? The situational compromises are the underlying assumptions. The underlying assumptions, and not the value systems, are the core culture. According to a former managing director and talent officer, Lehman's strong culture as a tough underdog guided managers to pursue over leveraged positions at Lehman (Greenfield, 2009).

Honesty and integrity in an organization are a legal requirement. Where is the option of even choosing it as a value system? It is legally binding on a business to have integrity. One must then ask: What prompts an organization to do so? Is that an admission of guilt? I believe that it is a classic Freudian slip.

Values are nothing more than an indication of an ideal world, if that. In practice, they are always negotiable, and, hence, there is nothing core about them. In confusing the values to be an actual driver of culture, organizations fool themselves, their employees and the entire ecosystem. So do organizations not need values? The short answer is that they do not. They need authenticity. Most values articulation turns out to be a poster that is inauthentic and unreal.

The aim of the core values for an organization seems to be brought down to looking good rather than being good. As long as an organization looks good and as long as it can make others believe that it looks good, they don't feel a need to face uncomfortable realities. I call these the pleasures of being taken care of in the ICU—the inauthentic culture unit. As the collapse of the Lehman Brothers suggests, the longevity of an organization is no indication of the institutionalization of any of its documented core values. Values are always vulnerable to reality. The reality is driven by leaders' interpretations and assumptions.

Research on strategic management shows that securing competitive advantage or making profits drives most of the decision-making in organizations. The term 'values' by definition implies the principles or standards of behaviours that are deemed important. Making money for an organization is a survival need. Why is it absent from core values? This is what inauthenticity means. Interestingly, Apple had 'setting aggressive goals' as a core value.

The problem with inauthenticity is that everyone sees it, and yet they have to pretend that what is documented in the inauthentic poster is important. They can't say that the values are inauthentic because that is an attack on people in leadership positions. Paying lip service to the ICU poster sets a boundary to be respected. Now what drives behaviour—the value called 'honesty' or the fact that no one can be seen calling the leaders 'dishonest'?

The assumptive boundaries are the real culture in an organization. The culture is not the values, mission or purpose. The real drivers of behaviour are the assumptions that people make collectively and largely. The reason organizations struggle with cultural change is because they rarely confront assumptions. They aim to change the values that were anyways unreal.

THE SUBTLE WAY OF SAYING
@#$% YOU

BEHAVIOURAL BOUNDARY SETTING

Across the world, organizational systems and structures are based on principles of reward and punishment. This has implications on how cultural boundaries are set. Rewards and punishments are not just tangible outcomes. The intangible ones often set the boundaries and assumptions. Let's say that you are at a party with your partner and you happen to crack a joke at the other's expense that everyone laughed at. Your partner laughs too, to appear a sport, but in the middle of it sneaks in a prolonged stare straight into your eyes. In that brief moment, the smile was replaced by a frown. What does that do to you? Do you make another joke? That is behavioural boundary setting. There was no reward. There was no punishment. Yet a boundary was set—there was no longer freedom of speech.

The reticent and indirect ways in which leaders reward or punish people set the tone for assumptions. Look at it as a binary reactive system. Any action, behaviour or initiation from one person draws a response from another. The response could be approval or disapproval. Approval can take the form of excitement, smile, verbal expression or a furtherance of one's suggestion into further discussion. This sets a boundary for what is acceptable to discuss. On the other hand, disapproval can have many forms too. These could be frown, ignorance, delays of responses, anger or rebuttal, silence or even lack of engagement in future. These set an even stronger boundary for what is unacceptable. Future behaviour is far likely to be governed by these boundaries, rather than by the documented code of conduct.

Just as in your school days, you knew which teacher you could openly talk to and which teacher you absolutely had to keep shut in front of; in the same way, people pick up leadership cues. The leadership cues set the tone for acceptable behaviours, norms, discussions, thinking and doing. These tones are the actual processes that drive the behaviour and are culture in action. For example, within a family, one instinctively knows the topics that can or should be discussed with one parent or another. That shared instinct sets cultural boundaries within a small eco-system. In a similar way, it does so in a larger one.

Leaders in an organization have their own priorities, agendas and deliverables. As we discussed in the previous stage, it sets in place a mechanism for making decisions for them. That context drives their judgement. Quite often then, knowingly or unknow-ingly, the context meets other members. The context reflects in the leader's approval or disapproval, verbally or otherwise. Repetitive reflections that are mirrored by other leaders set the boundaries of culture over a period of time. After a while, these boundaries operate almost like muscle memory does, where no one might know why things are done the way they are done, and yet everyone does them that way.

Authenticity takes courage. It is far easier to frown or cut off communications with things and people you don't approve of than to have an explicit and open conversation about why you don't. The explicit conversation implies openness to being proven wrong. That is a psychological journey that few under-take. Leaders are guarded; they want to look good, appear open, seem concerned, be a role model, be respected and all those things. People working for leaders in organizations have their own fears and insecurities, and so they feed the leaders with whatever meets their approvals, even if temporarily. In the end, this inauthentic dance sets in a culture within which the organi-zation works.

Can you imagine that in a 158-year-old legacy of Lehman Brothers, no one working with the CEO thought that they were over leveraged? The ones who did were probably sidelined, and the system was run by the CEO's close aides. As an analysis points out, the ones who strategically disagreed were scared to communicate with the executives on the 31st floor decision-making centre (Stevens & Buechler, 2013). These were bright people from the best of the business schools in the world. The documented culture was all about openness and trust. The behavioural boundary setting ensured that the managers were not allowed to speak up. The document was only a side issue. The boundaries prevailed. The assumptions ended the legacy.

DROP THE PRETENCE

DON'T BE ASHAMED OF WHO YOU ARE AND WHAT YOU STAND FOR

Confusion exists in choices, not in clarity. Very often, organizations are more worried about what they appear to be than what they are. Every single person in one of the big four consulting firms that I was consulting with wanted to project an image that was in line with becoming a partner. So everyone emulated what the partners would do—long working hours, indulging in conceptual debates, excessive focus on money and monetary benefits and high lofty personal ambitions. People's self-esteems were ruled by whether or not they would make it as partners. They made compromises on their personal lives, bought things they didn't need and advised companies based on what would prolong monetary benefits versus what might be the right thing to do. In the end, the people had very little clue about the human beings that they were. In their own words, they had become consultants. That defined them. The problem was that a majority of them led unhappy lives full of pressure and stress.

In another company in Mumbai, a market leader in an old economy industry, the management is unashamedly proud of being sales focused and that's what they value most. This company has over 50 per cent market share. The employees are old fashioned. The offices bear the look of a 1960s movie. The culture is totally hierarchical. The employees will fail all modern-day leadership assessment tests. They have no documented values, no written code of ethics and are governed by very tight micromanaged controls. Most of their managers will be unable to clear the first round interview in any decent company. Yet none of this bothers them. The shareholders and management of the company have deliberately kept out their own next generations from managing the business, because the next generation is image conscious. The authenticity works for them because no one is confused about what to expect.

A business has to be able to monetize the possibilities before it, and it has to be able to expand or generate further possibilities. What slows down the execution of either of these, or even impedes it, are confusing assumptions and boundaries. I was consulting with one of the leading advertising agencies in India, where the constant chatter and 'looking-good' feature was about ideas and creativity. At the back end, their constant decision-making was around revenues and profits. They were never comfortable in boldly declaring that intent. In the end, they lost both the creative people and the business people. The agency was eventually acquired by a global company.

What the leadership of a company truly values is reflected in their behavioural boundary setting to employees anyway. What they say they value becomes the confusing path on which their employees and ecosystems judge them upon. The gap between the two lands the company in an ICU trap where they may still be successful, but they will not be brilliant because they no longer have the momentum to do so.

It may be interesting to note that start-ups or early-stage growth companies, where they build market acquisition or when a story build-up happens in a company's graph, happens when they don't have a documented value systems, or a set cultural codes, or even any process bylaws. Once they get established, they build up all of these to look good.

In practice, authenticity prevails over appearances. People always know what lies beneath the appearances. As a company, either rise up to the appearance or acknowledge the authentic principles at work and make them the appearance. In the absence of this, it is like running an engine that is quite confused at all times that whether it needs coal or electricity. It does a bit of both and somehow keeps surviving. However, can this confusion ever become a brilliant benchmark?

POTENTIAL IS ALWAYS
GREATER THAN THE VISION

DIMINISHING POTENTIAL SYNDROME

We had discussed in the previous stage that potential is built up when the available energy is always ahead of the effects that are created. Effects or end results in an organization are pre-determined by the leadership. The development of people is then directed towards meeting the effects. Potential is, in a way, nurtured towards the goal. Organizations seem to view capability as function of its containment, that is, individuals within a company develop within the contours or the control of the organization itself. Professionally, even though this may appear to be the case for a majority of people, the argument is rationally unsustainable.

People get exposed to a variety of things, make interpretations, develop ideas and form perspective on things, continually. As a result, people have a different view of the effects that they can create. People's ideas about their potential impact interact with decision-makers, who are already committed to a certain impact. These ideas are judged, accordingly. Different perspectives exist over a period of time in an organization about the effects that the potential available to it may create. These should usually be the healthy conflicts to have. In practice, however, the behavioural boundary setting ensures that a lot of these conflicts are unaddressed. The unaddressed conflicts of these kinds become a reverse energy mechanism. That is, the energy available to disregard a potential effect becomes greater than the effect. This is the diminishing potential syndrome. Thereafter, if the organization thinks about doing something unique or different, it tends to believe that it doesn't have adequate skills.

The unaddressed conflicts in a system usually set the assumptions within which execution takes place. In other words, the potential of an organization gets limited by its ability to confront and address conflicts. A reputed HR director of a multi-billion-dollar organization recently told us that their management philosophy does not believe in developing leaders because they believe that they have a brand large enough to attract and hire leaders whenever they need. This view indicates that the organization largely views leadership as a necessary instrument to produce a certain effect. Therefore, when they need an effect, they will hire the leader who can produce it. On a closer analysis, we found that a majority of the senior management positions in the company were filled by outsiders. The company believes that it doesn't have to produce leaders and, therefore, believes that its people are not ready to be leaders. The unaddressed aspirations of the people emerged to be the top-most unaddressed conflict in this organization. Not surprisingly, the top-most strategy that gets executed in this company is a cost-driven focus on stretching bottom lines because no one believes that they have the capability to differentiate or think of a growth-driven strategy, otherwise.

Talent is a direct outcome of investment in capability. A high-performing talent in one company can simply be reduced to a nobody in another because of the cultural assumptions that exist within a system.

Culture is an outcome of decision-making and is not an occurrence independent of it that leaders seek to address through decision-making. The way the leaders derive context from the external environments, and shape the teams and individuals to meet the demands of the context, indicates the cultural journey. Within these specifications, leaders set strategies and reward mechanisms and inadvertently set behavioural boundaries that leave conflicts unaddressed. These unaddressed assumptions become the cultural spines which dictate action. Cultural change or cultural setting needs to first discover the assumptions before setting in a process of change because the change itself will interact with these roadblocks.

Smartphone ideas already existed in the mobile manufacturing companies before Apple took it on.

Search engines were a secondary function for web portals like Yahoo before Google made it its primary business.

Every large fashion house or retail company would have presented a plan to move operations online.

Airlines around the world persisted with a business model that shows declining profits.

There are automobile companies still in denial about alternate fuel and electric vehicles. The same might be the case for nations which rely on revenue through fuel.

People within each of these companies had and have alternate voices and conflicting opinions. The decision-making patterns, however, dictate whether they will even be addressed, voiced or not. It is not that the companies don't have the potential. They do. They probably don't have the culture to produce different results. They are bound by assumptions and behaviours that are unanalysed. Meanwhile, the values document looks like a 10/10.

CREDO

CULTURE CREDO: STRATEGIC EFFECTIVENESS IS CULTURE IN OPERATION

As you can see by now, strategy setting and strategy execution are derived and dependant on cultural roots within an organization. The great strategic moments that one sees or hears about in the press or books are not some brainwave realizations. They are an outcome of a culture. They are an outcome of a set of systemic assumptions.

1. What is your explicit value creation, that is, how will you discover and solve newer problems?

2. What is your explicit value capture, that is, how do you explain to everyone what you will achieve?

3. What is the exact environment (innovation or openness or bureaucracy) that enables this the best?

4. What is the exact role of leadership or of your senior-most leaders in enabling these?

5. How do leaders become aware of and address unresolved conflicts within your system?

6. How do you ensure that you are following the right map and not getting swayed by the context of any singular leader?

7. How do you reward people? Why do you reward them for what you do? What do your rewards signify, that is, what do they encourage people to do and to ignore? Is it the right way?

8. What behavioural boundaries do your leaders tend to set inadvertently?

9. What assumptions are driving your key decisions? Are these assumptions known and open to challenge?

10. Despite any prevalent structure within your organization, does the frontline have access to the leaders without threat and intimidation?

Organization strategy and culture are not two separate documents or codes. They are one and integral or one another.

REFERENCES

Greenfield, H. (2009). *Culture crash*. Conference Board Review, *19465432, 46*(5).

Stevens, B., & Buechler, S. (2013). An analysis of the Lehman Brothers code of ethics and the role it played in the firm. *Journal of Leadership, Accountability and Ethics, 10*(1), 43–57.

STAGE EIGHT

EXECUTION IS MOMENTUM

EXECUTION IS ALWAYS IN PROGRESS

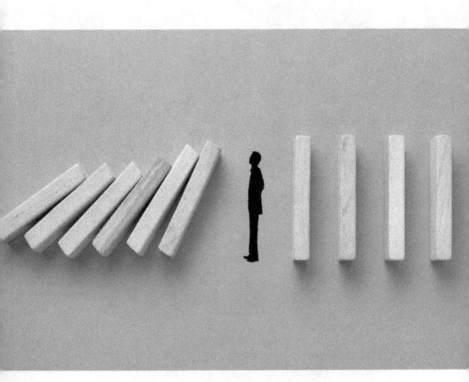

THE DIRECTION OF ACTION

A strategy implemented perfectly is execution.

A strategy implemented imperfectly is also execution.

A system working in absence of a strategy is also execution.

A person not knowing what to do and whiling away their time is also execution.

Execution is always in motion. There is nothing called as 'not executing'—everyone is always executing something. It could be in an entirely different direction than desired by the organization, but it still is executing. What is the real problem? Is execution the problem or direction of execution the problem?

Organizations take great comfort in blaming their ability to execute plans and tend to lean over towards the argument that execution may be a problem in their system. This is a simplistic digression and abdication of leadership. It almost amounts to saying that people in the organization come to work to not actually work. This is a very hollow and pessimistic view of the world. What does it say about your beliefs about people? And if that actually may be your belief about people, as a leader especially, then whose problem is it, yours or theirs?

The last few chapters we were discussing the case of the Lehman Brothers. Was that a problem of execution? Certainly not. Executives were busy executing a high-risk strategy. The ones who were against it were busy executing a strategy to keep shut to preserve their jobs. Was the decline of Kodak a problem of execution? Those executives might still be the best in the world at producing and distributing films. Is shutting down of retail stores such as Woolworths or Debenhams a result of poor execution? Was the collapse of Nokia and Blackberry from the pinnacles of market leadership a collapse of execution? Are these collapses about the inability to execute or more about the direction of execution itself?

Giving people goals to achieve and their inability to deliver on those goals is not an execution failure; it is a strategic blunder. The choice of goals, the choice of people, the choice of building capabilities in those people, the choice of accepting and rejecting suggestions, the choice of markets, the choice of pricing, the choice of product mix and the choice of available resources to make people successful are all strategic decisions that were taken by an organization's leadership. How on earth then is the non-achievement of goals an execution failure?

Blaming execution alone will digress the critical challenges that leadership must address. A statement like 'Our people are not able to execute plans' is a regressive generalization of issues. What does it mean? Do people not have the capability? Do they fundamentally want to fail? Why are they unable to execute? Is there something wrong with the plan?

People are always doing something. Action is rarely ever the problem. The problem is the direction of action. Whose responsibility is it to provide support, reward and monitor direction?

Direction of action is a fair indicator of the future. If you are sitting and watching news on television every single night, there is enough probability that you will be agitated and argumentative on most days. The reason is simple. Your execution was in the direction of consuming substance that achieves that and not in the direction of relaxing.

Similarly, the end result is a fair indication of the direction that was actually allowed by the system or people. If the end result is that the goals were left unachieved, then that implies that the direction setting was inadequate or inaccurate. You don't simply motivate people now to do more of the same thing. Instead, how about revisiting what you want people to do—how, what and why.

There is one exceptional circumstance when execution is actually a problem. People know exactly what to do. They know how to do it. They have the capability to do it. They know why they should be doing it. They understand the rewards of doing it and the consequences of not doing it. And they still don't do it. This is much like people not focusing on or neglecting their health. There is one plausible explanation for this situation— they just don't care. People just don't land at these points in their lives. They arrive at these points as a result of circumstances. In an organizational context, these circumstances are the culture, and as we discussed in the previous stage, the drivers are the leaders.

BUT WE DOUBLED THE RESOURCES

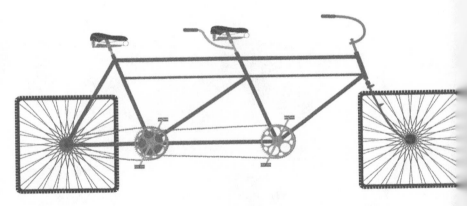

MOMENTUM EFFECT

If the organization is an object that must achieve a certain result in time, then the laws of physics dictate that it must be in momentum. Management science and theories unfortunately have not invested in understanding momentum. Understanding momentum is understanding execution.

Momentum is the measurement of the quantity of an object's motion. In physics, it is represented by a simple formula:

$$p = mv$$
$$Momentum = (mass)\ (velocity)$$

An organization, a system or even life is always in momentum, a favourable or an unfavourable one. The extent of achievement, in a sense, is an expression of scale and speed, that is, how much an organization could achieve and in what time period. This is essentially a goal-setting tenet adopted universally. How is execution related to momentum though? Let us expand the equation in management terms.

Mass for an organization would mean the physical mass in terms of people, resources, products, solutions, tools and processes, partner, customers, etc. This mass would combine together to produce a result. The result in an organization has to be time bound because the resource availability is not unlimited. It must produce a result to have access to the mass. Therefore, velocity becomes a key ingredient to success. The formula for velocity is *velocity = speed + direction*. Velocity is different from just speed. Speed is simply about how fast something moves. Velocity ascertains the object's speed and direction.

The word 'momentum' may well be replaced by the word 'execution' in an organization to understand achievement. If we do so, then execution is a result of how resources combine, how fast they move and in which direction. Three strategic levers then that determine execution would be the resources (and their abilities), the speed at which they move and the direction towards which they move. Anyone missing a piece in this formula will compromise execution. The problem is not execution; the problem is the missing piece.

You can have all the resources in place. Are they able and capable? Do they know how to combine, when to combine and when not to combine? Does your process ensure combinatorial success? This is actually the easy part of the puzzle, that is, to put the resources needed in place. How do you now build speed?

Picture an example of driving a car on the highway. Apart from the traffic on road, what determines your ability to go fast? There are five critical elements to build speed. Skill, practice, tools, security and fun. You, of course, need the skill to drive a car fast enough. The skill needs practice to hone; that is, you can go faster with practice. You need the right tools to enable you to go fast, for example, the car or the road. You need to feel a certain level of security at a certain level of speed. Speed is a risk, right? You need to be secure enough that you won't crash or that if you do, you will still be fine. And finally, it needs to be fun for you to drive the car fast or else you won't put in the practice required, will you?

Here are the critical questions that one must ponder over for building speed in an organization.

Do people have the skill and ability to go fast (much like the potential reservoir discussed earlier)?

Are they allowed to practise and develop their skills on a regular basis? Can they implement and play with their new learnt behaviours at the workplace, or are they judged for them?

Do people have tools to enable them to go fast? The tools could be technology, processes, support systems, culture, colleagues, teams, etc.

Do people feel secure enough to take the risks of speed? How are your reward and punishment systems aligned to this?

Speed is of course stressful, but is it fun in your organization? In other words, does stress of speed outweigh the fun of it or does the fun outweigh the stress of it?

Then there is direction. Execution is incomplete without direction. Which way is the organization headed? The clearer the direction is, the clearer the road is and the faster one can go. If the direction is unclear and the road map is not available, any amount of resources, tools and speed will fall short because they simply don't know how and where to get to. Similarly, if you have the right direction but inadequate or untrained resources, they won't reach the destination. Sometimes you have the right resources and right direction but may not have the right tools. A simple progression of tools, for example, the online travel booking engine, and a failure to adapt well to it, collapsed the world's first and oldest travel agency, Thomas Cook, after a mammoth 178 years in business.

KNOWING WHERE TO GO
IS NOT A STRATEGY

GOALS VERSUS STRATEGY VERSUS DIRECTION

Goals are mostly value capture intents. Most strategy-setting exercises in organizations are merely budget allocations or statements of intents. Neither budgets, nor intents are strategies, even though organizations tend to believe that they are. For example, a decision to expand geographically or to introduce new products or services is a goal to acquire newer markets but it is not a strategy by itself. Take a look at these two sets of questions.

Do you know exactly what value you will create, how and when will you create that value, and how you will go on enhancing and creating further value for your customers? Is this value creation solving unique problems in your industry, and do you know exactly how you will get potential customers to adopt your solution? Thereafter, do you have a systemic plan for capturing the created value?

Or

Do you know your value capture intents, that is, the milestones you have elected to reach in your growth journey, year after year? These could be the achievement or financial milestones that you have chosen. Further, do you have projections for different scenarios and budget allocations for acquisition of resources and future expansions?

The first set of questions is a strategy. The second set of questions is merely goals that the organization assumes is a strategy. The leaders in the second set will tend to blame 'execution' because in their minds the strategy looks perfect on an Excel sheet. In the first set, the leaders will have to correct the system for generating or capturing value based on performance feedback.

The simple test of goals and strategy is having clarity about value creation and capture, whereas usually goals setting seems to be merely expressing intents. A classic, practical example that exists in organizations around these is allocating sales quotas to sales teams. Based on past performance and future intents, for example, a sales target might be set to grow next year by 10 per cent. If you ask the leaders what their strategy is, they will tell you that their strategy is to grow the business next year by 10 per cent. The sales teams, of course, follow a tactical plan to meet these quotas. Tactics are important, but tactics are not strategy.

Directions, on the other hand, can take numerous forms, from broad to precise. A direction is a map to achieve the objective, that is, how to get to the destination.

The map executes the strategy or the lack of it and is always being executed in an organization. If that execution is not yielding the desired result, the solution is not to blame the executors but first to challenge the strategy that produced the map itself. Was that strategy ever designed to create a unique value before attempting to capture it? Was that strategy ever designed to enhance people's capabilities to create or capture a newer value? Was that strategy ever designed to solve unsolved problems? Or was that strategy simply derived from an intent, in which case the directions were based on the destination alone without knowing the road that leads to it.

Momentum is everything. How does your mass travel with speed in the right direction and towards the same direction? This unification is not just about having the same goal; it's also about having a strategy that encompasses the entire mass. Anything short of this is simply incompetent leadership.

BARRIERS TO MOMENTUM

Take a look at Figure 8.1. It captures the essence of a ripple effect of what is normally construed in organizations as troubles arising out of execution.

Execution is an effect and not simply a means to an effect. This one realization can enable organizations to fix problems when they occur. Let's look at the seven barriers that produce an inverse effect on execution.

1. *Unclear direction or strategy:* When the direction setting is unclear, vague or purely goal centric, it has an adverse motivational effect. Setting high lofty goals, on one side, can be associated with positive anticipations, however in practice, if not backed with clear strategies and executable directions, will lower the motivations of people and create an insecure environment. It impacts execution because people don't have an answer to their 'how to's' and often are even fearful of seeking answers.

2. *Poor cross-functional communications:* The mass of an organization is a build of teams. In the absence of strategic alignment, people tend to build their own relevance. This establishes structures and power centres that may not always combine well. Poor alignment leads to higher-than-needed bureaucracy.

3. *Bureaucracy:* While moderately needed to ensure checks and balances, bureaucracy affects speed. Speed often misses deadlines and milestones.

4. *Speed:* is a key element of momentum, as discussed earlier. The motivation, as result of bureaucratic goals, becomes misplaced between the importance of teams and the organizational goals. Execution becomes a victim on accounts of mass as well as velocity.

5. *Inadequate delegation:* The above-mentioned realities usually force managers and leaders into protecting themselves and

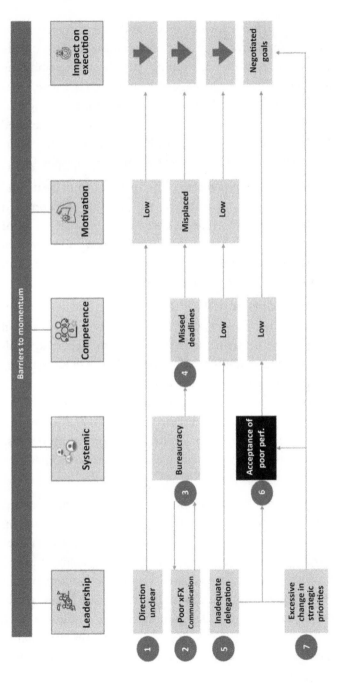

Figure 8.1 Execution Barriers

covering up for a loss of speed and target achievement. They get motivated to produce fewer mistakes. This usually takes their eyes off developing people and establishing their own relevance. Managers may tend to delegate inadequately, resulting in lower team competence and motivation. Execution suffers because the mass is not developed adequately, lacks appropriate leadership tools, and managers and leaders become bottlenecks for picking up speed.

6. *Acceptance of poor performance:* The inability to delegate and develop capability effectively has another outcome. It produces poor performance. Once poor or relatively poor performance becomes a norm across teams, the levels of competence for the organization as a whole drop. This often leads to excessive changes in priorities.

7. *Excessive changes in priorities:* A drop in performance forces managers and leaders to view capability and execution ability as a constraint, and they tend to negotiate goals and strategies much more. It is much like a spiral reaction. The goals that were set were not achieved, the competence was lowered, and now the new goals are negotiated. This basically means that the distance to be travelled is lowered; however, it still may have an effect on momentum because the intent to lower the distance was not to build momentum, it was to avoid building it.

The strategy or the lack of it can have multiple levels of effects within an organization and, in the end, everything reflects on execution. That something didn't happen because it wasn't executed offers no insight because it is an accurate statement in any context. Why it didn't get executed requires a candour within leaders that few organizations seem to possess. This partly explains the reasons why leaders popularly view cultures as resistant to changes. The change is often required in the way leaders behave, rather than the way the rest of the organization reacts.

EDUCATED TO BE SELFISH

CONNECTION BETWEEN EXECUTION AND ORGANIZATION'S BELIEF SYSTEM

The way the leaders of an organization think, the way the goals are articulated and the way the conversations around these take place in the organization impact whether the organization will be a pacemaker or a floater. As the names suggest, pacemakers tend to be the future drivers and floaters tend to be the ones that are a part of a Red Queen's race.

If the organization is primarily interested in value capturing and tends to have a higher focus on making money, then its systems are usually very monetary centric. They tend to motivate people through money as a prime instrument. The excessive focus on wealth and money beginning with the shareholders and leaders trickles down to the entire ecosystem. These organizations end up educating and training everyone to think 'money' first. In the end, the people emulate that philosophy. Naturally, their own desires of money and benefits outweigh the larger concerns or problems that the organization may be trying to solve.

On the other hand, a problem-focused organization which is looking to solve new problems and create better solutions or products is driven by solving the problem rather than the money. The highs in this structure tend to come from identifying problems and thinking about solutions. Here, the people get educated towards handling concerns, and these concerns outweigh monetary desires. It is this organization which is more positioned to be the pacemaker, or have the GQ.

Both these systems execute the priorities. In their extremes, none is workable, of course. However, as was cited earlier in the research on strategic intents and creative outcomes, the problem-focused organization has been observed to create far greater value than the profit-centric one. While we were discussing speed earlier, the element of fun was mentioned as a component of creating speed. While making money may be fun, an excessive focus on constant money comparisons at a daily level is more stressful than fun. It is here that these cultures hit the speed ceiling, whereas in solving problems even a little amount of progress alleviates the stress that existed before it.

Another way to examine this is that a vast majority of scientific breakthroughs and academic theories that go on to win Nobel Prizes are developed in cultures and institutions that have very little to offer in terms of monetary benefits. This is not to suggest that an organization must take its eyes off financial success. Rather, it is to suggest that it must lay focus on solving problems and creating value that will produce financial success as an outcome, anyway.

BRILLIANCE CREDO

The root causes of ineffective execution will almost always never be as simple as 'we are bad in execution'. The real question is why it is a problem. Here are a few questions to help you clarify and get to the root of the real problem.

1. What are the tasks that need to be accomplished to reach your goals?

2. Are the tasks of all the functions aligned into a strategic road map?

3. What knowledge and working style will help an individual win with the task?

4. Do people's strengths match the tasks they are expected to accomplish?

5. Are capability development and time therein parts of your execution plan?

6. Is knowledge built into your customer connection?

7. Is knowledge built into your value-creation and capture process?

8. Is knowledge built into your cross-functional collaborations?

9. Given your overall business strategy and the scope of your products or service offerings, what core capabilities do you want to invest in?

10. If momentum $= mv$, where are your roadblocks, specifically?

11. Which leadership issues do these roadblocks signify?

12. What organizational beliefs does this uncover?

13. What is your plan to address it?

BUILDING THE STRATEGIC BRILLIANCE MAP

THE ELEPHANT
IS ALWAYS IN THE ROOM

CAN YOU DEVELOP AN EMBARRASSINGLY SIMPLE STRATEGIC PLAN?

We attach complexities to problems, rather to the problems or situations that we perceive to be complex. The reality mostly tends to be embarrassingly simple—so embarrassing that we can't not act on it.

When we perceive reality (e.g., life) to be complex, we look for complex solutions or, at least, overlook the obvious simple ones. Within an organization, complexity is 'socially' perceived as acceptable, else why would one need managers and leaders, right? We are forced to look for the complex solutions because the simple one has no benchmarks, no examples. This is evident in the fact that most of the management case studies are written with intriguing dynamics at play that management students are to learn from.

No candidate you interviewed ever told you that he or she wants to do a simple job and, in all probability, neither did you ever tell anyone that you have a simple job for them. That is probably the reason why we find it more difficult to implement the simple. People attach 'statuses' to things and are then compelled to make decisions for getting those. These things include cars, houses, lifestyle, marriage, kids (all things we call 'settled') and, in an organizational context, these simply translate to numbers of all kinds. We attach so much value to these (unknowingly) that when it comes to crunch time, we choose to get convinced about the option that is 'socially' correct. We do this because if we fail, we'd rather fail with a correct complex option than a simple obvious one. This is inherent; we are brought up to live this way. This is a trap that everyone falls for. For those people who work in firms and are shaking their head in disbelief, allow me to develop a simple model from strategies adopted by Gandhi.

Let us take an example from the life of Gandhi to understand this. India fighting for freedom from the British rule was a complex situation for every Indian. Gandhi's simplification (a) was that British ruled the Indians because Indians chose to be governed by the British and to achieve freedom, one had to reject that choice. Gandhi uncovered the conflict in the minds of people where freedom was equated to fighting, and they could not perceive defeating the British army for obvious reasons. Non-violence as a strategy (b) was an embarrassing simplification. Gandhi didn't blame or complain about anything. (c) He executed his solution whether or not the people accepted it.

Before we start building your strategic brilliant map in this final stage, let's first introduce you to a method for simple solutions. This has just three things for you to do. Consider them a quick checklist to determine if a solution is simple or not.

1. Accept that we perceive reality to be complex (even when it is not), but the solution is going to be embarrassingly simple or it is not yet solved.

2. Every reality has a basic 'conflict' that needs to be uncovered.

3. Blaming or complaining about another person or problem or situation takes us further away from the simple solution and takes us closer to making peace with complexities.

This book, thus far, has introduced the reader to many concepts. It is time now to integrate those concepts into a simple, strategic framework. It is my hope that you are able to use and apply the framework in creating a brilliant plan for yourself. When you do, remember the three rules mentioned here and apply them to every step of the process. In the end, the solution has to be as obvious as an elephant in the room. The reason that this is brilliant is because it takes a brilliant mind to take a problem and convert it into a solution which is simple enough for anyone to adopt. Adoption of a solution is most often the key to actually solving a problem.

Complexity is amazingly addictive. People and organizations create perceptions of complexity to their environments. It gives them a sense of relevance and a whole lot of occupational significance. Complexity cannot have a fast growth; simplicity can.

STEP-1
THE TWO I's

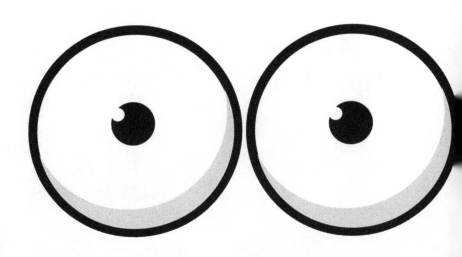

THE INNER GAME OF BRILLIANCE

Stages 1 and 2 of the book largely discussed the inner game of brilliance and creativity. There are conflicting demands upon leadership as there are upon life. These conflicting demands, for example, a demand to remain financially secure versus a desire to take ambitious risks, present choices. The way we perceive the needs to these demands in the context of our lives and organizations determines the choices we may or may not make.

Brilliance is not about the outcome. It is first an inner game, much like the life of a sportsperson, where the outcomes on the field follow the rituals of developing an inner game off the field. The inner game produces the outer result eventually.

The inner game of brilliance can be understood with the two Is formula, and it is the first step in developing the strategic brilliant map. The first I is 'integration'.

Stage 1 narrated the framework for the whole picture, that is, the distributive dimension which was an integration of different views. Throughout this book, we have laid emphasis on the 'and' factor and not on the 'or' factor. Integration is the 'and'. Integrative thinking is not about compromises or choices. It is about collaborative approaches and absorption of all choices. It is not about 'risk versus security'; it is about both risk and security. Mathematically, the integration symbol means or represents a continuous sum of the quantities. That is exactly what integrative approach is—an ability to continuously represent the wholistic dimension and to continuously strive for the potential of the 'and' rather than the 'or'. The integrative solutions are not evident immediately, and it is important to realize that the process of maintaining an integrative approach is not about always knowing the solution, but it is more about persevering until it is found. This is where the second I becomes a part of this inner game. The second I is 'intent'.

Stage 2 discussed a direct correlation between strategic intent and creative outcomes. It was noted that the intent of discovering real problems, rather than the problems of securing competitive advantages or problems related to making money, has the greatest effect on value creation. Being brilliant is being ahead on the problem curve, that is, solving problems that other players are not even considering yet. Doing this in a manner that is an integrative or a continuous function creates an organization that is always ahead of the curve.

I refer to 'integration' and 'intent' as inner games because neither skill is taught in our education systems and is largely left to the individual to develop or discover. The autobiographies of champion sportspeople such as Pete Sampras, Sachin Tendulkar, Michael Jordan, Pele or Muhammed Ali have a common thread. Each of these champions invested years full of painful, laborious hours on first developing the game itself and not on dreaming about the awards. That is intent—finding a way to up the game. In business language, that is about creating value that solves a problem and ups the standard of an entire industry. In organizations, the intent has to move alongside integration because organizations are a team dynamic. Teams and people will always have conflicting views, thoughts and ideas. In the 'and' dynamic, like Mr O's solution, no one loses. It is when everyone wins that brilliance comes upon.

Simplifying even further, 'intent' is building an inner game where

Concern > Desire.

And 'integration' is building an inner game where

Concern is wholistic and continuous.

Once the two Is are understood, the rest of the map becomes infinitely easier to create. The summations of the two Is combine to provide a strategic foresight. This foresight will guide the entire map to follow; therefore, it is crucial that we dive deep into discovering the two Is.

Take a moment to document this foresight. This is not choosing between a goal and a purpose. It is about integrating the reflections you made in the various brilliance credos in this book into a foresight that captures both your concern and your desire.

THE BLUEPRINT

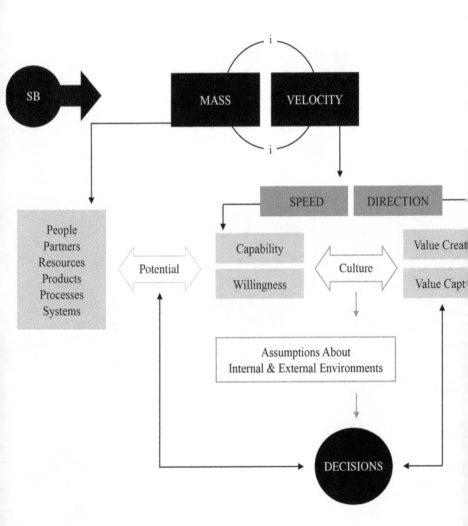

LET'S SIMPLIFY STRATEGIC BRILLIANCE

The graphic on the previous page summarizes this entire book and presents the template for creating a strategic brilliance map. Let's understand that this is a whole and dive into the specifics to help you create your map.

In the previous stage, we discussed momentum and execution as a function of mass and velocity. Combining integrative thinking and intent as continuous and overarching foresight into that formula give us a road map for strategic brilliance.

Step 1: The Two Is—What Is Your Foresight?

Strategic foresight is a combination of integrative thinking and intent to discover and solve problems. Most goal and vision statements in organizations are limited to a value capture intent. Cultural journeys and strategic execution then typically run in an organization as two separate movements. In the end, the intent dominates and defines an unspecified culture. The objective here is to develop an authentic foresight. Leaders often get consumed in articulating a concise vision statement that looks pretty and appears lofty. Why do they have that particular vision is a question very few will answer convincingly. If we apply integrative thinking to strategic foresight itself, then strategic foresight must be a combination of at least the following elements:

- What are the unique unsolved problems that you have discovered that need to be solved to create and add value? (Refer to Stages 3 and 4). (Note: Unique means that the problem discovered is unique to you, and no one else is solving it currently.)

- How do these problems integrate with the business side of your organization?

- What value do you aim to capture while solving these problems?

- What is the integrative dimension, that is, what kinds of problems or a mechanism to identify problems will you discover continuously such that you can be ahead on the problem curve?

Do this first: Answer these questions and combine them to document your strategic foresight. This strategic foresight will guide the principles of mass and velocity to create brilliance. Don't move ahead to the other steps without having a strategic foresight, because you must know what you are about to execute before making projections and plans to execute.

Step 2: Direction Setting

The entire strategic activity in a business can be directionally conceived as value creation and value capture. These are two questions:

- What value and what unique value does the business create?

- How does the business capture value from the market?

Value creation (refer to Stage 5) is an outcome of problem identification and discovery. When we apply the two Is to it, the business must also explore how it will continue to identify unsolved problems and stay true to the intent of applying the lens of 'problem discovery' to making decisions. Value capture, on the other hand, is what dominates most organizational goals and strategies. The value capture mechanisms usually land us in a Red Queen's race situation. However, the continuous value creation may ensure that the strategy will not get caught in that circular race.

Do this first: Refer to your strategic foresight document and break it into the value that the organization needs to create or can create (not about who and how it will happen right now) for different stakeholders. These could be customers, partners, employees, shareholders, environment, society, governments, local communities and others. Creating multiple avenues of value creation is integrative application. Apple, for example, follows a deliberate strategy to expand its ecosystem through partners and app developers. This ensures multiplicity of opportunities to capture value in return.

If this value is created, what possibilities of capturing that value in the form of revenue or profits or social capital or goodwill exist and in what probable time scales?

Does the value captured ensure that value creation can go on to be a sustainable and scalable activity? If not, then creation is not simplified enough for adoption and needs to be rethought.

Step 3: Mass—Who and What Do You Need to Make Creation and Capture Happen?

I have always found it amazingly ridiculous that organizational structures in companies are not a part of strategy setting. It is almost usually a separate human resources exercise and is mostly aimed at governance and administrative controls. This approach is in defiance of the first I of the two Is principle—integration. Thereafter, most organizations complain about execution problems. The mechanism itself is incompatible with strategic execution. The very structure that is supposed to deliver the organizational strategy is not built around the critical and directional questions of value creation and value capture.

Mass of the organization refers to its people, partners (or the extended ecosystem including customer, distributors, developers and franchises), resources (assets, finances, intellectual properties, knowledge, etc.), products or solutions, and processes and systems that govern the mass itself. The objective of the mass is to achieve the directional setting in terms of value creation and value capture. Every component of the mass must fit into one of these two objectives, directly or indirectly, or else it is a waste. It is a waste because that particular mass is stationed and not in motion towards the strategic foresight. It slows down the entire system.

From the deliberations of Step 2, there are questions that present themselves for conceiving or structuring the mass.

- What are the tasks required to be done for value creation and value capture across all stakeholders as conceived previously?

- What components of the mass are these tasks attributed to?

- What composition of mass or teams are most likely to succeed in creating and capturing value?

- What support structures will make them successful?

- How will you match the strengths of the people to the tasks?

- What leadership styles will enable these individuals to succeed?

- What knowledge capabilities will help the individuals win in their tasks?

The mass is needed to accomplish tasks. It is pertinent that strategic goals are broken into tasks, and structures are determined rather than structures dictating the tasks.

Do this first: Based on the above questions, attribute the mass to the tasks such that the direction setting looks like an obvious reality.

Step 4: Speed—Can You Do It Faster than the Norm?

How quickly can actions translate into results? Comparative to other organizations that you may compete with, this particular question is a key metric. Can your mass achieve the same level of output faster? If yes, you have a competitive advantage; if not, then you have competitive baggage.

Speed is an outcome of capability and willingness.

That is as an individual.

Do I have the ability (and resources) to go fast?

And am I willing to go fast?

Velocity, which is an outcome of speed and direction, indicates that speed has to be built towards the direction in Step 2. An organization must build and develop its capability in the direction of enabling people to create more value and capture value. The test of capability acquisition in the metric of speed is the mass geared up to achieve results faster; that is, do they accomplish their tasks in quicker time than the industry average?

Further clarity on this particular discussion requires another dimension to be brought into this particular discussion and that is Step 5.

Step 5: Potential—Energy Is Always Ahead of the Effects

In Stage 6 of this book, we had discussed potential as the available ability to create an effect being greater than the effect itself at all times. Therefore, capability development must ensure, on the one hand, that current capabilities are producing the effects faster and, on the other hand, that future capabilities or knowledge acquisitions are always available as a reservoir of potential towards the objectives of creating and capturing value.

The strategy for speed has to ensure that

$$\text{Energy} > \text{Effect.}$$

The effect being produced is faster than the competition, still and in the direction set in Step 2.

Do this first: Answer the following questions before you move to the next step.

- Given your overall business strategy for value creation, capture and breakdown of that into the scope for the mass, what core capabilities do you need to invest in to ensure the objectives for speed?

- What role will this knowledge acquisition play in the value you create for and from your customers and other stakeholders?

- How and to what extent are you or can you invest in building up potential (and for which mass) such that the energy reservoir is always in surplus?

Step 6: Culture—The Underlying Truth

The sum total of your approach in building the strategy map thus far is already culture in motion.

Stage 7 outlined the cultural intricacies at play in an organization. Culture is a set of underlying assumptions about the external environment, the individual, teams and their relationship with organization's strategy and rewards. Culture in this manner produces results.

In practice, culture gets knotted up in conflicts of what leaders feel is nice to project versus what is really needed to be done. Once the culture loses authenticity, everyone is confused. Confusion doesn't produce execution because confusion stalls speed and, therefore, momentum.

- What assumptions are you making about your internal and external environments towards value creation and value capture?

- What are the real 'keys' to your success, and are your strategic objectives (Steps 1–5) documented authentically and without false appearances?

- How are conflicts addressed (or not), raised (or not) and settled (or not) in your C-suite? This is usually a fair indication of your culture.

- What are people rewarded or punished for, not just monetarily but also in terms of status, power, praise and access? People's interpretation of the underlying culture is a direct outcome of this.

Do this first: Based on your assumptions about internal and external environments that will produce the result, answer the questions on Stage 7 brilliance credo and then the following:

- How do you want individuals to behave? Which behaviours are critical to your strategic direction?

- How do you want the teams to behave? Which behaviours are critical to your strategic direction?

- Is the organizational strategy in line with these behaviours?

- Are your reward mechanisms, performance management systems and capability developments aligned to these behaviours?

- Are your leaders role models and flag bearers for these behaviours, or what behavioural boundary setting (Stage 7) needs to be challenged and examined?

Step 7: Decisions—The Ultimate Unit of Analysis

The challenge that faces an organization is again keeping the two Is alive, that is, the inner game of brilliance. In Steps 1–6 exists a strategic map, but the question that will come upon leaders is whether it sets an integrative context or a selective context for them. The context determines decisions (Stage 6). If the inner game of brilliance is a conscious approach in leaders, then the decisions are likely to be in sync with strategic brilliance. Eventually, everything converges upon the decision and subsequent execution. Therefore, the clearer and more authentic the strategic boundaries are, the clearer is the decision-making process and outcomes.

Here are some questions that can help you identify whether your mass is making the right calls.

- Is your leadership bandwidth required to make unnecessary and repetitive decisions? If so, then what gaps in the culture exist and are not fixed?

- What level of clarity about strategic blueprint is required at different levels of management to enable them to make the right calls independently?

- Does your culture support making the right decision with ready contingency plans? Or is it safer for people to not make decisions?

- Does your mass feel secure enough to take decisions, and are they clear enough in direction to take calls?

- Have you gained the commitment and the capacity of resources who will convert the decision into action?

- Are their mechanisms in place to provide feedback and encourage and manage arising conflicts?

EPILOGUE

EVERYTHING EXPIRES

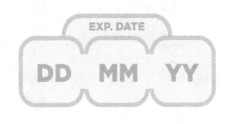

THE ENEMY OF YOUR BRILLIANCE IS YOUR BECAUSE

We all have ideas.

We all have intelligence.

We all get inspired.

We all have potential.

We all have moments of brilliance.

Everything expires. Everything is perishable.

Like all perishable things, they perish if they are not used in time.

Ideas, intelligence, inspirations, potential and brilliance are no different. If it is put on the shelf or stored in a 'tomorrow' cupboard, it will expire.

Inspiration and motivation can tend to be magical. In that moment, when you receive it, it really is. And then it goes away. It will always go away if it is not used.

The enemy of inspiration is this word in your head called 'because'. I won't or can't or not right now or it's not the right time because…. Regardless of what you add beyond the 'because', whether true or untrue, it is the death of an opportunity for brilliance.

A majority of readers never read an entire book they buy. If you have reached this page, you are in the minority already. No matter what your situation in life is, you have been presented with enough ideas, concepts and advices to create momentum. It is a wonderful thing to get motivated and inspired. It will only work for you though, if you take action and not find a 'because'. I hope that you will find it in you to put yourself in an even greater minority by taking action.

Inaction sets an expiry date on knowledge, even from your own memory.

Put your brilliance to work so that brilliance can work for you. Action sustains and converts knowledge into multiplicative effects.

THE

AND

WE RiSE
BY LiFTiNG
OTHERS

COMPASSION VERSUS ECONOMICS

Unpredictability is the very heart of success. Oftentimes, we can anticipate but not predict the outcomes of our decisions and actions, especially in business. We want our strategies to succeed, we plan for it, we execute them and yet we may or may not see the results. The certainty of outcomes is always imperfect. It is this uncertainty that itself presents opportunities for change. The future will bring even more unpredictable change at a breakneck pace.

Economic results are usually an outcome of a business model combined with other elements, as we discussed in building strategy maps. Leaders make choices to decide each and every component of the map. People join organizations for various needs and largely follow the direction set by the system. They may question the direction, add value to it or reposition it, but in the end, the direction or let's say the negotiated direction is largely a given.

That direction produces economic results or the lack of it. Either of the economic outcomes may make the leaders greedy or anxious for more. It is here that they begin to lose compassion. This could be compassion towards their employees, customers, society, or their realities and needs. The loss of compassion is justified through economic compulsions.

Once the relevance for economic outcomes becomes greater than the compassion, people begin to follow or abide only for their own economic security or greed. Leadership, in this moment, is dead. Leaders become number-driven slaves. The system becomes a binary slot machine which is judged and thrilled purely by the coins it throws out.

As we had discussed earlier, this system takes little time to become negatively creative to produce money. Negative creations could be in the form of negative decisions or impact on the culture, on the elements of the mass, on capability building or, most importantly, on the two Is—intent and integrative thinking.

These businesses may still make money, enjoy profits and, therefore, a question may be asked that what is wrong with it? The answer is simple. It is against the laws of nature to not be compassionate and, therefore, it becomes unsustainable, much like in the cases of the Lehman Brothers, Enron and alike. The boundary lines within an excessive economy-focused organizations are blurred, and the leaders end up with the ramifications of decisions that they no longer will be able to handle, sooner or later.

That is the final 'and' of brilliance. Yes, we need economic success and growth, and yet we need compassion. How does one choose in a conflict of economic survival versus a compassionate existence? The answer is integrative thinking.

If the business model has reached a stage where it is compelled to take uncompassionate decisions, then the reason for that stage is already misdirection. The same thinking cannot solve the problem.

An article in *The New York Times* recently noted that high-powered, financial-focused corporations are breeding grounds for greedy behaviour. The excessive need for economic successes in organizations causes financial stress in people's mind. The American Psychological Association reports, year after year, have shown that financial issues remain the most salient stressor for their respondents and have adverse effects on mental health (American Psychological Association, 2019; APA Task Force on Socioeconomic Status, 2006). The collective effect of this system is bound to be unsustainable itself. This is not a matter of 'if' but 'when'.

Compassion is the key to integrative thinking and solution finding. It is also the key to establishing the intent beyond an economic mindset. Both the two Is are non-existent without compassion.

There may not be a possibility called brilliance without there first being compassion. At the etymological roots of the word, compassion means to understand suffering of others. Problem discovery begins with compassion. The lack of compassion discovers greed. Interestingly, the word 'intelligence' means the faculty of comprehension. What one may comprehend, whether greed or concern, may well be the foundational difference in the intelligence that creates brilliance.

REFERENCES

American Psychological Association. (2016). *Stress in America: The impact of discrimination*. Stress in America Survey.

APA Task Force on Socioeconomic Status. (2006). *Final report: APA task force on socioeconomic status*. American Psychological Association.

ABOUT THE AUTHOR

Chetan Walia delivers the combined value of an experienced global business strategist, senior advisor and facilitator to Fortune 500 companies, Asian firms and global family-owned businesses on how to build and manage strong, global brands as well as leadership of high-performing, marketing-oriented businesses in a hyper-connected and fast-paced, digitalized world.

He has almost 25 years of experience working strategically with businesses and with the C-suite. He is also a research scholar and publishes in various academic journals and conferences. He is pioneering the academic development of the creative strategic perspective.

Chetan has published books about strategy, leadership, breakthroughs, success and growth.

In various other avatars of life, he is or has been a photographer, entrepreneur, restaurateur, copywriter, graphic designer, publisher, academic researcher and mediator.

INDEX

STAY **ENCOURAGED**
STAY **CREATIVE**
STAY **MOTIVATED**

Keep abreast of the most cutting-edge thinking driving businesses today.

   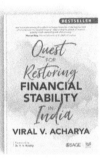

www.sagepub.in